A Life Given in Love

Reflections on Philippine Duchesne

A Life Given in Love

Reflections on Philippine Duchesne

Edited by

Juliet Mousseau, RSCJ

Society of the Sacred Heart

St. Louis, Missouri

A Life Given in Love
Reflections on Philippine Duchesne

Edited by Juliet Mousseau, RSCJ

Book design by Peggy Nehmen, n-kcreative.com

ISBN: 978-0-9971329-3-9
Printed in the United States of America

On the cover: Sculpture representing Saint Philippine Duchesne in the garden of the Cathedral Basilica of St. Louis. Sculptor: Gianfranco Tassara of Inspired Artisans, Milwaukee, Wisconsin.

Published by:

 **Society of the Sacred Heart™**
United States – Canada

4120 Forest Park Avenue
St. Louis Missouri 63108-2809
314-652-1500
rscj.org

Contents

Zeal for Mission

Courage

Philippine As Our Guide

Introduction

How **DO ANY OF** us come to know other persons—not just know about them, but know them, know what captures their imagination, what dreams they cherish, what serves as their lodestar, and what keeps them going in the ordinary time of their lives? We want to know, too, how they deal with sufferings and disappointments of every kind, what breaks their heart, and what gives them hope?

Knowing another person becomes markedly more difficult if that person lived many years ago, as did Rose Philippine Duchesne, to whom these reflections are dedicated. To come to know Philippine, we must rely on a variety of sources.

There is the legacy of her accomplishments: schools and communities and the numbers of professed religious and novices in the country at the time of her death. Even more important is the gradual spread of the Society of the Sacred Heart to more than forty countries around the world because of one woman's passion to cross the Atlantic to bring God's love to the New World.

Written documents are a wonderful source of information about Philippine, most notably the recent publication of her complete writings in French and English, only now being mined for insight into this complex woman. There are some brief biographical snippets of those who encountered Philippine. There are journal entries written by those who were part of her community, recording significant moments in their common life.

There is also a rich oral tradition available to us, stories passed down among those who knew and loved Philippine, stories sometimes "improved upon" in the transmission. Was it pebbles or feathers or leaves that her beloved Potawatomi placed on the hem of her habit? Does it matter? Or does the story—if it happened at all—simply illustrate the Potawatomi admiration for her profoundly contemplative presence among them.

A Life Given in Love offers glimpses of the life and legacy of Rose Philippine Duchesne. Beginning as a collection of homilies, it was expanded to include a poem and a prayer, a conference, a letter, some essays, a "three minute loving colloquium," and even the imagined advice of Philippine to the writer. Many authors are Religious of the Sacred Heart, but the reflections of others also fill these pages, including an archbishop, several Jesuits, and some members of the Sacred Heart family—alumnae, faculty and friends. Each writer is briefly identified at the end of the book.

Given the varied background of the writers and the different genres they chose to shape their reflections, *A Life Given in Love* is organized lightly around six themes.

A first chapter offers elements of Philippine's biography, glimpses of her early years, her family's prominence and politics, the ways the French Revolution shaped her choices, her "extravagant heart for mission," the frontier world that greeted her, and her unwavering courage in establishing and expanding the mission and the community in the midst of setbacks and hardships of every kind.

A second chapter includes reflections about the friendship of Philippine with Saint Madeleine Sophie Barat, founder of the Society of the Sacred Heart, who welcomed Philippine into the community, formed her in the ways of prayer, and remained faithful friend and soulmate for thirty-four years even when separated by an ocean. Theirs was an unlikely friendship, so different were they in background, class, temperament, and spirituality. But they were bound together by a common desire to glorify the Heart of Jesus and to make God's love known. These pages portray the impact of friendship in living the holy life and remaining faithful to one's calling and mission.

The vocation of the Religious of the Sacred Heart has been called "wholly contemplative and wholly apostolic." Contemplation and apostolic activity are two discrete but inseparable realities. A life of prayer, while grounding one in God, also impels one to the service of others. The many needs of those served drive one back to prayer. Chapter three includes reflections on Philippine as "the woman who prays always," the title given her by the Potawatomi. As one essay concludes: "prayer sculpted her into Christ." At the same time, prayer clearly fueled her intense apostolic life, the theme of chapter four. She was mission-driven and filled with burning zeal, two words often used to portray her. She was intolerant of half-way measures, a woman of graced stamina and heart-driven intensity. Hers was a heart on fire.

A fifth chapter has the theme of courage, a Philippine attribute underscored throughout the book, but here in greater relief. The etymology of courage is, after all, in the Latin *cor*, heart, and we would be hard-pressed to name another so wholehearted as she. Courage marked her convictions, her choices, her unwavering strength to persevere in the face of uncertainty, suffering, darkness, even failure—the latter a word she often used of herself in times of opposition, discouragement, and loss.

Philippine's physical and moral courage in the face of doubt and uncertainty is a model for our world today. The final chapter considers the many ways she has been and remains a model and guide. She spent herself to make Christ known and loved. She crossed frontiers, both geographic and existential, to embrace the mission God's grace implanted in her heart. She was single-minded and single-hearted despite bouts of self-doubt. As one author points out, ours is a time that can use all the models of "strength, endurance, and patience under trial" that it can get.

Indeed, the reflections assembled in these pages are not an exercise in nostalgia, a bicentennial backward glance at a woman we have come to know and love. They are offered as Philippine's summons to each one of us in the family of the Sacred Heart to live a life of holiness, to zeal for the works of God, and to boldness and courage in the face of difficulties of every kind.

Let Philippine invite us all to *A Life Given in Love.*

Kathleen Hughes, RSCJ
March 21, 2018
Anniversary of the day Philippine's journey to America began

Biographical Reflections

Telling Our Stories

Juliet Mousseau, RSCJ
November 18, 2017

As we grow up, we learn about who we are through stories. The stories I heard growing up were of many sorts. I learned about my ancestors: the ones who came over on the Mayflower, the families who packed up their belongings and went west to Oregon, my great grandparents who landed at Ellis Island from Slovakia and made a home in New York, the Oregon lumberjacks who came from Sweden. I read the novels by Laura Ingalls Wilder, which gave color to pioneer life. As a young child in Montana, I learned about Lewis and Clark's expedition (which passed through the mountain behind the one I lived on), and about "the four Georgians" who gave the future site of Helena, Montana, "One Last Chance" and struck gold, founding my hometown.

These stories taught me to value an independent spirit, hard (and even backbreaking) work that would bring me to my goals, and a self-reliance that is built on living far from our nearest neighbors. While my family wasn't extreme by any means, I learned that we were on our own, not exactly isolated but certainly independent.

When I began exploring religious life, I met Philippine. As I learned the story of her life, bits and pieces of my personal story became wound up in hers. Just as she moved away from her home to Saint Charles, life far from loved ones was ingrained in my own history. We speak of her as a frontier woman and pioneer, which matches the imagery of Laura Ingalls Wilder's stories. Elements of my family identity stories are woven into Philippine's life, too: the Lewis and Clark Trail begins from down the street from her Shrine; and she was a personal friend of Father De Smet, who worked among the Flathead in Montana.

As I learned about Philippine, my values and the stories that made them part of my life took on different meaning. Instead of the individualism and independence that is so often valued in our American culture, we find in Philippine a distinctive holiness, one that comes from focusing her hard work and attention on others rather than on her own goals or desires. Instead of disconnectedness from those who were far away, we see a woman who sought always to be communicating with Sophie in France, and whose heart broke when her letters went unanswered.

As noted by Cathy Mooney, Philippine found her joy in serving Christ through others. Her work was not for the sake of accomplishment, but rather for the sake of relationship and community. She was working for the reign of God that Isaiah speaks of! So, Philippine's adventurous spirit and hard work weren't for her own gain, or even to bring success to the Society of the Sacred Heart. Her eyes were always on the needs of the children in front of her. She came to North America to find the peripheries, the frontiers. When she landed, and Bishop Dubourg asked her to teach the white children who had no access to education, that's what she did. Though she longed to teach the Indian children who didn't know Jesus, she went where she was sent and devoted herself to the mission there. She lived in Saint Charles, where people worked hard and sought the American dream. Philippine put her heart and soul into meeting the needs of these children in this place. To me, this says that she was entirely focused on doing the work of God, even if *her* hopes were not being met in that work. Doing God's work, and being with the ones who needed her, was what truly mattered. As we quoted above, "It is my happiness and glory to serve my divine Savior in the person of the unfortunate and the poor"—and the uneducated.

This fundamental attention to the needs of others is at the heart of our Christian faith. The God we believe in is a Trinitarian God. Just as the Trinity is a communion of relationships, so also we are called to live in imitation of that community in our daily life. Pope Francis speaks to this in *Evangelii Gaudium, the Joy of the Gospel,* when he asserts that the salvation of each individual Christian is bound up in the salvation of us all. God saved us as a community, and so we live intimately connected to one another. Pope Francis says: "The very mystery of the Trinity reminds us that we have been created in the image of that divine communion, and so we cannot achieve fulfillment or salvation purely by our own efforts. . . . Accepting the first proclamation, which invites us to receive God's love and to love God in return with the very love that is God's gift, brings forth in our lives and actions a primary and fundamental response: to desire, seek and protect the good of others" (*Evangelii Gaudium* 178).

This reflects the same image Sophie Barat had in mind when she started the Society in 1800. She felt a responsibility to the well-being of the people of France as they recovered from the violence and suffering of the French Revolution. In bringing together children (mostly girls) who lacked an education and especially a Christian education, she wanted to form them to be good people, caring for one another, and shaping the future of the nation. Through their human formation among the Religious of the Sacred Heart, it was hoped that they would influence the world around them for the good. As Isaiah was called to do, they were to rejoice in God and comfort God's people, to bring hope out of the ruins of their cities. The work of rebuilding a nation was to begin in the education of the children, which had been neglected in the midst of such suffering.

It was Sophie's hope that this little work of the Society, educating the children, would have a profound impact on the world as a whole, beginning with the nation of France. With that hope for a changed social reality in mind, Sophie sent Philippine to the American frontier to build up a nation that was perhaps too focused on self-promotion and bootstraps mentality. Sophie and Philippine show us what it means to radiate the love of God in our world, so that God's love can transforms what it touches. Again, Pope Francis speaks of this process (*EG* 9): "Goodness always tends to spread. Every authentic experience of truth and goodness seeks by its very nature to grow within us, and any person who has experienced a profound liberation becomes more sensitive to the needs of others. As it expands, goodness takes root and develops."

As American Catholics in the twenty-first century, what stories do we value? What values do we pass on? In this world, filled with violence, discrimination, division, and individualism, can we be a voice of hope and transformation? Like Philippine, can we attend to the work of God that is placed in our care, and leave behind our concerns about success or failure, being liked or being scoffed at, winning or losing? Once we can see that our salvation is bound up in the salvation of everyone else, we will truly be able to say, "How beautiful upon the mountains are the feet of those who bring good news, who announce peace . . . for the Lord has comforted the people, our God of love has redeemed us. All the ends of the earth will see the salvation of our God" (Isa 52:7, 10; 49:13 *New Revised Standard*).

Slip Us Your Secret[1]

Odeide Mouton, RSCJ

BY WAY OF INTRODUCTION, this is not a homily. It is only a three-minute loving colloquium with Saint Philippine Duchesne of an old pupil of Grand Coteau, the first house she founded after opening Saint Charles. Indeed, at Coteau, one became familiar with Philippine's bold bullseye target for the lowest and most enervating services to be given.

It would have been a delight to see her expression, if people wear expressions in heaven, when the celestial news broke there of her approaching canonization.

What are you telling us today, Philippine, our happy saint?

With what astonishment, what amused wonder did you see the universal church recognize that in you God has done great things?

You who loved so strongly, so tenderly, will you quietly slip us your secret, so that we too become women of prayer who are aflame to give the substance of our life without compensation?

You who treated and allowed others to treat you as the last and least, to what humility will you draw us in joyous self-effacement?

And what are you telling us about friendship, you who loved it so profoundly?

And of suffering born in silence?

And of your preferential solicitude for the most abandoned on the American mission scene, the American Indian?

Saint Philippine, our sister today in glory, speak to our hearts, so clearly, so plainly, that it will be impossible for us not to hear you. Whisper to each one of us what holiness the spirit calls her to. And if we never attain your austerity, may your prayerful sisterly affection win for us the grace to rejoin you in love.

When I read this three minute colloquium to someone in preparation for this liturgy, she said, "You must add a little story to implement some of this." But that shatters my

---

1 From an audio recording housed at the USC Provincial Archives, Saint Louis, Missouri.

three-minute introduction. However, as we are heralding all of Philippine's virtues, here's an opportunity of obedience for five additional minutes of your attention.

In the colloquium I spoke of Philippine's love as strong and tender. I think I can encapsulate in these few additional minutes, a rarely heard story of Providence giving Philippine a striking opportunity to exercise her strong and tender love for her father.

Pierre François Duchesne, her father, was a lawyer of repute, a sterling member of the political group of the *haute bourgeoisie* and a Voltairian. Today, he might be qualified by the expression *Catholique non pratiquant*, a euphemistic cliché for the clever French, hatched, matched, dispatched: a Catholic whose church presence includes baptism, marriage, and funeral. We know that he extricated his daughter Philippine at the end of her years of noviceship, insisting that the times were not healthy for priests, nuns, and churchgoers. Indeed, his concern for his family motivated his moving them out of Grenoble to their large country home in Grâne.

All conventual houses were confiscated. The nuns there were required to forsake their vows or else leave the country. At Grâne, Philippine took over the family chores. She even nursed her mother through a lengthy terminal illness.

An interesting insert here. At the mother's death, Philippine became an heiress. She was the oldest member of her family. She promptly distributed the greater amount of her inheritance to her married sisters and set aside a fund that would enable her to obtain the use of Sainte-Marie d'En-Haut after the Revolution. Then Philippine did her pioneer mission in social service. She rented a small house near Sainte-Marie. Sainte-Marie had become a prison for those who were to be guillotined. Despite the danger, she secured food for them, also hosts and wine for the interned priests. She also gathered the little French urchins running the streets, hungry and in tattered garments. She taught them catechism, inveigling them by promises of food and some clothing.

Shortly after his wife's death, Mr. Duchesne's health failed. His doctors informed him in early 1814 that he had but a few weeks to live. He became an invalid in his house in Grenoble. When this news reached Mother Barat, she wrote to Philippine, that despite the structure of cloister for female religious and its strictures, Philippine was not only to visit her father, but to spend some days at his bedside, caring for him. His married daughters, concerned about his Voltairian and irreligious stance, began to storm heaven for his conversion. The young grandchildren who loved their *bon papa* prayed every day, seeing the grief of their parents, that *grand-papa* would decry the vain philosophy, enemy of our religion.

Philippine's extraordinary presence for several days was heartwarming for all of them. In this certain intimacy with his daughter, Pierre François Duchesne, having experienced his oldest intransigent daughter, possessing an abrasive temperament, recognized the child who most resembled him and recognized in her competent care, which he was now experiencing, that from such a character would flower greatness and even beauty when human excesses were corrected. In his daughter that intransigence issued in doctrinal firmness. That power became Christian virtue. When he brought up his erroneous metaphysical stances, Philippine quietly refuted them individually. He was proud of his daughter, admiring her intellectual and moral qualities.

In his lengthy insomnias, the old politician read over his past with Duchesne reflections, and one fine day he announced that he now believed in the immortality of the soul, in the redeeming Christ, in the God of mercy, in the church founded by the Redeemer, and that he desired to receive again the sacraments of his youth. Following his reception of extreme unction, the married daughters took over the nights with him.

The frankly Voltairian group of his friends was amazed at his open insistence before them of the depths of his conversion. At his death on the 29th of March, they prepared striking obsequies of Voltairian burial. On the same day, 20,000 Austrian troops, friends of the royal couple, marched into Grenoble, so the Voltairian obsequies never took place.

Perhaps all of Philippine's miracles didn't await the process of her canonization.

Philippine's Spiritual Growth

Judy Vollbrecht, RSCJ
November 18, 2009

THE LITURGY FOR TODAY'S feast presents us with two readings. In the first, a young man chooses to give his death away, rather than betray the God of his ancestors. In Saint Philippine Duchesne, whose life we celebrate in this liturgy, we see a young woman who lets go of all she knows and loves to give her life away in a foreign land.

The gospel shows us the differences in the way servants of a king use the gifts he gives them to produce greater riches, with the result that they are given a part in the kingdom. In Philippine, we see an old woman who has spent her life to extend the kingdom of God, and as a reward is invited to give her death away in the heart of the paschal mystery.

We can see her life through the prism of the stages of spiritual growth we have explored today: the child, the student, the householder, the forest dweller, and the holy beggar.

The Child: Philippine was born into a prosperous family in France in 1769.

The Student: At an early stage, Philippine was given the gift of an attraction to a contemplative life and service of the poor. She loved hearing stories told by missionaries back from America, and her heart burned with the desire to work with the Indians there.

She met Madeleine Sophie Barat in 1804 during the Society's first years. She gave dramatic expression to the joy in her heart. She kissed Sophie's feet, and exclaimed, "How beautiful on the mountain are the feet of those who bring good news of peace!" This was the beginning of a strong friendship based on their ardent love of God and passionate desire to bring God's love to a world infected with Jansenism and even to the ends of the earth.

Mother Barat shared Philippine's longing to go to the missions and hoped Philippine could go for both of them, but at that moment she needed her in France. For twelve years, Philippine immersed herself in the spirituality of the Society and its mission in France. Then, one day, Bishop Dubourg came from Louisiana to beg Mother Barat for missionaries. Philippine again threw herself at Mother Barat's feet, begging to go. This time the answer was yes.

Philippine becomes a householder: Mother Barat named Philippine superior of the small band that set sail for America in 1818. They landed in New Orleans after a horrible voyage, only to find that Bishop Dubourg hadn't made any arrangements for them or left them a message. More waiting. She learned to live in the present moment as they shared the loving hospitality of the Ursuline Sisters.

The first house of the Society of the Sacred Heart outside of France was in Saint Charles, Missouri: a seven-room cabin. Water froze in their buckets on the way to the house from the river; food froze on the table; they often had no fire because they lacked a saw to cut the wood! In spite of her fierce love of poverty, Philippine recognized that they could not fulfill their mission in such surroundings.

The next year they moved to Florissant where they had a convent, novitiate, boarding school, and free school. Hardships continued, but Mother Duchesne insisted that the Rule and customs of the Society be followed as faithfully as they could be and so preserved the unity of the Society. By 1828, she had founded six schools for the young women of Missouri and Louisiana. Twelve schools had been opened by 1850.

But Philippine always felt that she was a failure. She never learned English well, so she couldn't teach the American girls. She tried to establish free schools for Indian girls, but they didn't last. She wrote to Mother Barat, "I carry in my heart a great fear of spoiling things wherever I shall be, and this because of the words I think I heard in the depth of my soul: You are destined to please me, not so much by success as by bearing failure."

Philippine's missionary heart still longed to go to the American Indians. She enthusiastically supported the Jesuit missionaries who came to Florissant in 1823, and in spite of all the community lacked, she found ways to give them small gifts for their missionary work. She was especially close to Father De Smet, who always visited "good Mother Duchesne" when he returned from his Indian missionary trips. He considered her the greatest protector of their Indian missions.

The Forest Dweller: In 1840, Philippine was allowed to resign as superior of the American Mission. That same year, Father Verhaegen asked the Society for nuns to open a school among the Potawatomi at Sugar Creek in Kansas and insisted that Mother Duchesne be among the group. "She must come," he said. "She may not be able to do much work, but she will assure success to the mission by praying for us. Her very presence will draw down all manner of heavenly favors on the work." She was seventy-two when she became a "Forest Dweller."

Philippine never learned the Indian language, so she couldn't teach. She wasn't strong enough to do the hard mission work. She let go of *doing* in order to *be*—through prayer and small acts of kindness. She spent hours every day kneeling motionless before the tabernacle—sometimes she even spent the night.

Legend has it that some children decided to check this out. One night, as she knelt in the little chapel, they put some kernels of corn on the hem of her habit before they went to bed. Early the next morning, they crept back and found them still there! This amazed the Indians, and won their love and veneration. They called her "The Woman Who Always Prays."

Philippine was happy at Sugar Creek, but the realists of the mission saw her getting weaker and her health declining and, after only a year, persuaded Mother Barat that she should return to the Saint Louis area. That was probably the hardest obedience Philippine ever had.

The Holy Beggar: The last ten years of Philippine's life were spent at Saint Charles, in poverty, suffering, and prayer. "I feel that I am a worn-out instrument, a useless walking stick that is fit only to be hidden in a dark corner," she wrote. In Florissant earlier, she had chosen a narrow closet under a staircase as a sleeping room. Her small room in Saint Charles was almost as small and poor.

She was more highly esteemed and venerated than she imagined. She was almost transfigured by Holy Communion. A wonderful light was seen to shine from her face, as if a flame were reflected on it. The children used to wait reverently to watch her come out of the chapel after her thanksgiving.

Philippine died on November 18, 1852, at the age of eighty-three. She is a model for us of someone who lived through the stages of spiritual growth. May we learn all that she has to teach us!

Philippine Duchesne and the Changing Times

Margaret Williams, RSCJ
November 15, 1987

SISTER HELEN MCLAUGHLIN SAID to us in her last letter (Letter to the Society, May 1, 1987), "Philippine has surprised us by stirring the surface of our consciousness with extraordinary energy; she is saying something to us with urgency and insistence." Those very words make us think of Philippine: energy, urgency, insistence. What is she saying to us?

The document of the Chapter of 1970 concluded with the words: "Times change, and we too must change and modify our views." They were written by Madeleine Sophie to Philippine in 1831, and now make us wonder whether time ever does anything but change. It moves on and on and is a challenge to our own times, which are changing with the same speed as in the beginning. But perhaps these same words have created a stereotype in our thinking. Do we picture Madeleine Sophie as the enlightened progressive and Philippine as the die-hard conservative? Are these descriptions exact? It is well to look back into our history and ask: was this the wisdom of Madeleine Sophie checking the impetuosity of Philippine, or was Philippine the one who was rushing ahead and was told: not so fast? Or can it be that both Madeleine Sophie and Philippine were like ourselves, torn only too often between loyalty and vision, loyalty to something that we know is of God and vision that moves us into the unknown?

So, in the light of the coming canonization of Philippine Duchesne, it may be well to look again at our beginnings, remembering the warning of Janet Stuart: "Epochs of transition must keep us on the alert; they ask us to keep our eyes fixed on distant horizons. A beauty fully unfolded is ready to perish, so let us not rest in our beautiful past. It will remain true to the end that, as Cardinal Newman has said, 'Here below to live is to change, and to be perfect is to have changed often.'"

Looking back, what do we see? We see two remarkable women of contrasting temperaments interacting in a remarkable friendship, a friendship built on trust and love, made stronger by the fact that Madeleine Sophie was superior general, ultimately responsible for her friend's actions. Their stories cannot be separated, and yet they lived together for only four out of forty-eight years of experience made mutual through a difficult correspondence.

What of the years before they met? Even then, the keynote of Philippine's temperament was heart-driven intensity. She was born into tumultuously changing times, for the French Revolution is a watershed in human history. In her home, the values of the past were in conflict with the urgency of the present; her father stood for a movement estranged from the Church, and the child's loyalties were shaken to their very foundations. Then in the quiet of a monastic school, she heard a foreign missionary talk, and her own consciousness was shaken. She could never again be the same, because something was calling from the outside world. Yet she chose instead to enter a contemplative order, and then came the challenge of waiting. Her vows were put off year after year, and waiting was, for Philippine, the hardest thing to bear. Then she was thrown into work for the underground church, while not understanding the liberalism and democracy that were turning her world upside down. She tried to control events, obtained the use of her battered old monastery, and again waited while everything went wrong.

Here we meet a question not easy to answer. What was the real source of Philippine's personal difficulties? Was it that others simply could not feel with her intensity? Or was it something in herself that invited criticism and led to alienation, even dislike? Or was God taking his mission into his own hands? Helen McLaughlin says: "Philippine's openness to the Spirit, and the freedom of her whole being responding to his call, did not lead to great success, but rather to the deep experience that the grain of wheat must fall into the ground and die that the Lord may bring forth the harvest." That text comes to mind whenever we think of Philippine, and perhaps it answers our question.

We love to linger over the moment of her meeting with Madeleine Sophie, who stepped out of a carriage, found herself in a low, damp, corridor, peered into the dark and saw someone whirl towards her, drop at her feet and kiss them, saying: "How beautiful on the mountains are the feet of those bringing peace." And: "I let her do it through sheer stupefaction at the sight of such faith!" At once these complementary spirits fused to the point of union. They had much in common: passionately loving hearts, boundless desires, and unstinting gift of self. But they were also dissimilar. Madeleine Sophie, of frail physique, envied Philippine's robust health. Philippine's boldness chafed under the quiet prudence of Madeleine Sophie. One had the outward vision that looks beyond the horizon, the other the inward vision that seeks the center. And so fortitude met wisdom in the two wonderful leaders who shaped the Society to be always strong and wise.

For in a sense the Society was built upon this friendship, which rested on a shared call. Madeleine Sophie knew before she met Philippine that the Society was to go overseas. In 1804 she received a letter from Madagascar asking for recruits. Her answer was obvious:

not yet. But she said: "I knew when I read that letter that the Society was destined to cover the earth, and this thought struck me profoundly as a call from God." She knew that she could not answer it herself, but someone else had also heard it. She wrote to Philippine: "Have I given up my project? The same desire increases every day, and I have been asking that one of my companions may carry it out, and that the Spirit's own self may guide and lead her." The interpersonal mystery was at work: one person may carry out another's vision.

For the next ten years Madeleine Sophie fashioned the restive Philippine for her mission, guiding her in "the battle that you are waging with your own nature." Philippine's theme song was: "May I stay up all night and pray?" The answer was: "Get six hours of sleep!" It cost Madeleine Sophie to say that, for: "The silence of the night is certainly the best time for prayer. I know it is!" As for Philippine's other desires: "How can you expect me to approve your plans, each one more unreasonable than the last! ... What need you have of guidance! But that's enough; you are dear to me, so I cannot pass over your faults. ... I have need of your courage. I do not share your faith that you can walk over the Atlantic Ocean. Wait till I can find you a boat."

Then the great decision was made, and Philippine got as far as Bordeaux where she had to wait again. It is revealing to see what was on her mind during those hectic days of waiting on the wind. She wrote to Thérèse Maillucheau: "I am treasuring the vine slips that you sent me." Vine slips were to bear the grapes of old France in a new world, and Philippine nurtured these signs of continuity. Then there was the problem of daily living, and she wrote: "I have already made a great advance in changing my diet. I had never before eaten seafood!" Then, out of the blue, she pressed Mother Barat: "You did not answer my question. May we take day students?" Day students! They were expressly forbidden by the Constitutions; in the *pensionnats* "no day students are to be admitted." Had Philippine an intuition of this contingency in a new country? It was a leap in the dark, and this idea came to her at the moment of sailing! She was ready not only to change with the times but to restructure education! Philippine took day students from the beginning; in Europe the first day school was opened in 1852, the year of her death.

Philippine was utterly impersonal in meeting new situations. Immediately upon landing she wrote a long letter to the children of France with fascinating descriptions of what she saw: the changing color of the Mississippi waters as they enter the ocean, the strange trees along the shore. Then comes the first hint of a loss of—shall we say illusion? To give up an illusion is the pain of following a dream. "I have already seen the savages for whom we made this journey. They are poor, ignorant and sinful people." Do we recall her picture of the innocent children eager for God whom she had seen in her night of prayer at Sainte-Marie? And now she shrank from the ignorant and sinful outcasts seen in the streets of New Orleans. She wrote later: "At close range what seemed to be a beautiful reality is only a beautiful dream." Her dream had been Rousseau's philosophic notion of "the noble savage," then current in Europe.

To learn the truth Philippine became an avid reader of newspapers, getting information wherever she could. Sometimes her information was not quite accurate, as when she wrote to Mother Barat: "A certain missionary has told me that he has found the greatest similarities between Hebrew words and the Indian language, and he thinks that the Indians are descended from the Hebrews."

To help her in the difficult decisions that she now had to make, Philippine waited eagerly for letters from Mother Barat. When they finally came, they must have been hard reading. They were often very short: her friend could hardly find time to write in the rush of affairs at home. Philippine's outcry for help was answered with a repeated: "Don't ask me; I have no money, no people to send." It broke Mother Barat's heart to write in this fashion. "I am tormented by your position." "Check your impetuosity, your gifts." "Why are you not near your mother?" Then something still harder to read: "Why did you do that?" "Was that wise?" "At this distance, how can I judge? . . . Make your own decisions." The theme song of Philippine's letters now changed. She could pray all night without asking, instead she implored: "Take me out of this! I'm no good as superior." And the answer was always: "I have no one else. Keep on."

We now reach Madeleine Sophie's letter about the changing times. Philippine was low in spirits. Things were going wrong in Saint Louis; the house was badly run, the garden was a sight. (How different from Eugénie's houses down south!) She wrote to Mother Barat: "The Americans do not understand me, and the Creoles want good looks and attractive manners. The best thing for me to do is to disappear." At the same time, letters from other people were complaining of Philippine's want of management. Finally, Mother Barat wrote to Philippine, reluctantly, on November 30, 1831. "I cannot help being worried by the present condition of your house and by the small success attained in Saint Louis." She then devised a plan: let Mother Thiéfry be superior at Saint Louis, and let Philippine retire to Florissant and be as she longed to be. "God forbid that I should blame you, dear Mother, but times change, and we must change with them and modify our views."

But before Philippine could receive this letter, Bishop Rosati intervened. He wrote to Mother Barat: "There is no religious whom you could designate who could take Mother Duchesne's place." She must not be changed. So Philippine took up her burden again, until Mother Galitzine came ten years later and all too willingly let Philippine hide in a corner. At that moment came the call to the Indians. Philippine was with them for a brief year, then found herself again in a small room at Saint Charles. "God alone knows the reason for this recall" was her only comment.

What were her attitudes toward the changing times in the country that she tried so hard to understand? First, she rejoiced to watch the spread of the Church. "In this free country Catholic institutes prosper." It excited her to hear that a Catholic chaplain was appointed to Congress. She was very open to ecumenism. "Our priests fraternize with the ministers of other religions," and "We have more non-Catholic than Catholic pupils." She saw the American Church as a patent extension of the Kingdom of God on earth.

Regarding the American people and their customs, her reactions were mixed. She was shocked that Americans would not allow games on Sunday, but: "This is a Protestant country, and we must conform." She was astonished at the custom of sleeping with the windows open. "Americans enjoy drafts and push their beds near open doors!" (Perhaps sleeping under a staircase was not too heroic for Philippine!) She gave reserved admiration where it was due: "The people of the United States are remarkable for their care for external forms, their keenness of intellect and their genius for science and art. They have a passion for grandeur and knowledge. How can we change the attitude of a whole nation when it is supported by the natural bent of human beings? . . . Class distinctions are repugnant to the American character." And finally: "No nation on earth admires itself as this one does!"

The question of race relations was two-fold; Philippine faced the status of the Indians and that of black slaves. After her first shock concerning the Indians, came outrage at the way in which they were treated by the American government. She wrote often of the injustice that was driving them west, and she followed the work of the priests devoted to their welfare with avid sympathy. In the manner of slavery, injustice was not so obvious to her. It is helpful for us to realize how hard it is even for a saint to rise above the *status quo*. Slavery was accepted, even by Catholic bishops. Philippine wrote: "In this land of liberty it is very hard to get help in our work. We don't want slaves and we have no money to buy them, but we can't get along without them." So the Society of the Sacred Heart bought and sold slaves. What shocks us today as a profound moral evil was then a custom taken for granted, and Philippine was concerned with the happiness of individual black people.

In considering the current of prayer that ran through Philippine's life, we find a ready fidelity to the call of the Spirit as she was led her through changing times. Prayer was always a constant force in her life, and its essence did not change. The Indian children gave her the name Quah-kah-kah-num-ad, the woman who is always praying, but she had been a woman of prayer from the start. At school she had risen early to pray with the nuns, and she craved the life of a contemplative order. When Madeleine Sophie removed the grilles from Sainte-Marie, Philippine spent the day in tears. "Oh, my dear grilles!" "Your grilles, my dear," came the answer, "think no more of them. Our intentions and our actions cannot be shut up behind grilles."

For twelve years before Philippine's departure for America, Madeleine Sophie guided her towards contemplation-in-action, in letters filled with warmth, love and intimacy, redolent of the Song of Songs, mystical in tone. They reached a profound depth of sharing: "I have so great a desire that you should love Jesus that I don't even consider myself, because I want to pass into your soul the love and confidence that I should have for him, so that you can love him for me." When Philippine went overseas, the change in tone in Mother Barat's letters must have been very hard to bear. "I have said nothing to you about your soul; my brother will do it for me." And a letter from Louis followed. It was no longer possible to express the old intimacy under the pressure of distance, time and business, and so: "The Spirit of Jesus must give you his counsel."

Philippine was badly in need of reassurance. She confided to Madeleine Sophie: "I carry in my heart a great fear of spoiling things wherever I may be, and this because of some words I think I heard in the depth of my heart: 'You are destined to please me not so much by success as by failure.'" Again, when directives concerning the use of the Ignatian methods of prayer were given by the Council of 1833, Philippine wrote: "One difficult point is this emphasis on methods and examen. You told me once that you had the same difficulty and that consoles me. ... These new directives frighten me. I have never been able to reflect on a subject. I see it as a whole, and what I have once seen I shall see for ten years."

At Sugar Creek, with nothing to do but pray all day, Philippine found the contemplative depths to which she was called, realizing to the full the salvific value of pure prayer as well as of contemplation-in-action. And when recalled to Saint Charles: "I love my solitude, and I would love it still more if I had more of it." The road had not always been hard. "When I meditate on the fact that I belong to our Society, my soul expands with joy and tears of gratitude flow. I see only happiness in privations. Could God do more for me?" She found that she had friends who loved her deeply and with whom she was at ease. They were found especially among her old novices, Regis Hamilton, Gonzague Boilvin, and Anna Shannon.

It is sometimes possible to catch glimpses of God's ways with his outstanding lovers. Three illustrations of his pattern with Philippine appear in the stories of Aloysia Jouve, Anna du Rousier and Suzannah Boudreau. Philippine was not aware of these patterns; they are revealed in the history of the Society as it moves on with the changing times.

Aloysia Jouve was Philippine' niece and was formed by her aunt while a child at school at Sainte-Marie. Madeleine Sophie had high hopes of what this gifted person, with her deep spiritual insights, could do for the Society, and Aloysia herself longed to go overseas. Philippine wrote: "Form Aloysia for me; she is young enough to learn Chinese!" Instead, Aloysia died at the age of twenty-four, in France. At Mother Barat's urgent request her life was written. When it was read to the novices at Grand Coteau, a sixteen-year-old postulant named Mary Ann Hardey was so inspired that she asked to change her name to Aloysia. As Aloysia Hardey, she later founded twenty-five houses stretching from Halifax to Havana, an outstanding educator and administrator, carrying out the unfulfilled desires of Philippine and Aloysia Jouve.

Anna du Rousier was at school in Poitiers when Philippine, on her way to America, stopped there and spoke to the pupils. She told them of her mission, of which she knew nothing, then said: "Which of you would like to come and join me?" Hands waved excitedly, but Anna sat still. "At that moment," she said, "my vocation changed from Carmel to the Sacred Heart." She entered, and experienced tragic failure when the houses in Piedmont were closed during the revolution of 1848. Mother Barat then sent her to visit the houses in America. She reached Saint Charles in time to receive the blessing of the dying Philippine. "I shall always feel that cross on my forehead," she said. She did not go back to France but on to South America, opening another continent to the Society.

Suzannah Boudreau was the child of a poor family whom Philippine educated in gratitude for what her father had done for the house at La Fourche, and whom she received into the Society at the age of fourteen. We know Philippine's way of looking beyond the horizon. While at Sugar Creek she wrote to Madeleine Sophie: "Here I feel the same longing for the Rocky Mountain missions that I experienced in France when I first begged to come to America, the same longing that I felt for the Indian missions once I had reached this country. They say that in the Rockies people live to be one hundred years old. As I am only seventy-three and my health is improving, will you not authorize me to go farther west?" Instead she was recalled to Saint Charles; another was to carry out the vision seen at Sugar Creek. In the meantime the Indian mission moved to Saint Marys, Kansas, where it struggled on until forced to close in 1879. Mother Lehon, then superior general, said: "The closing of Saint Mary's enables me to accept a foundation in Timaru, New Zealand, for it has freed enough personnel: the foundresses will leave from Saint Louis." Suzannah Boudreau was then vicar and sailed with the colonists. She reached Timaru in January 1880, saw the laying of the cornerstone of a new convent, and died within twelve days. The Society, by sailing "farther west" had reached the far southeast. The pattern is always the same: waiting, failing, moving on.

Madeleine Sophie was left without her dear friend when Philippine died in 1852, but she expected the pattern to unfold into the future. When a call came from China in 1858, she said to the probanists, and to us: "I have had to refuse and my heart is heavy, but subjects are wanting. When there was question of America, I did not hesitate to send Mother Duchesne, for I knew that she was according to the heart of God. And now that the harvest is so great, can I find no one of whom the Master wishes to make use to do great things?"

The Vocation of Philippine Duchesne for the Missions

Saint Madeleine Sophie
recounted in the Novitiate Journal of Kientzheim, 1852

I ARRIVED IN GRENOBLE, at the Monastery of Sainte Marie d'En-Haut where Mother Duchesne herself received me.

She was always an example for us through her exact observance of the Rule. However, there was still something that she did not yet understand about our vocation: it concerned the salvation of souls, and it was on this point that I knew I had to persist. How to reach this soul so strong and generous without hurting her, and I assure you that I was watching for any opportunity. It was not that she was lacking in zeal—that she had. But she confined herself within her own walls. She did not understand that we wanted to reach out to the whole world, as far as possible. She kept within her own little house, of course very suitable, and to her little garden, which was for Philippine, who looked only for God, her whole universe. She did not understand that to draw souls to Our Lord a much vaster enclosure was necessary.

I used to see her only once a month when she would come to speak of what was in her heart on the day of her monthly retreat. She would never take even a half-hour, too scrupulous to lose time with useless words. She said what was necessary, then would leave. I admired her conduct, but I assure you that it upset me at times: I would have so loved to have her more expansive; I wanted to open my heart to her, to speak together about God, since I could not do so with my other sisters, even though they were very good, but still so young, almost children; yet it was impossible and I could not detain her.

One day, however, when she came as usual to speak of her monthly retreat, I was singularly inspired by the Spirit of God to risk a little. It was God who wanted it so. When she had finished, and I was giving her a little advice, I opened my heart to her on a point which always remained on my conscience. In my youth, almost since my childhood, I had read the life and letters of Saint Francis Xavier and always since that time the desire of the foreign missions stayed in my heart, even though I had no idea how that would ever happen, since our Society did not even exist, nor was there any idea of it. Later, when it was formed, I spoke openly to Father Varin about this desire, and he replied that it was not God's design for me, that I was destined for France. I submitted without understanding the meaning of these words, because we had only our little Paris house; but I submitted. Nevertheless, I carried a longing in my heart that could not be entirely satisfied. Well, at least, if I could find a soul who would replace me who would sacrifice herself for the foreign missions, I would be content and feel better. ... Mother Duchesne listened to me, said nothing, not a word, then left like lightning, as was her way.

I did not see her again until the following month. This time she spoke directly and said that she believed she was that soul, that the reason that she had not replied at the time when I spoke to her was that it had been impossible for her, so struck was she. "Since then," she said, "I have reflected a great deal before Our Lord. I believe," she added, "I have recognized his will, so use me accordingly. You have only to speak. I am ready."

I replied that the moment was not yet, since we were so few, and that I needed her but later we would see. It is thus that I made her wait for ten years, during which time she did not stop asking me. What prayers, penances she made to obtain this grace. It was through many sacrifices, through the practice of severe mortification that she prepared herself for this difficult life, which she led later on in America.

A Vessel of the Spirit

Rosemary Bearss, RSCJ
Excerpts from a Lecture on Philippine Duchesne
Bicentennial of the Society of the Sacred Heart
Carrollton School of the Sacred Heart
March 15, 2000

Introduction

A FEW MONTHS AGO I was watching a replay of a documentary on Leonard Bernstein directing the New York Philharmonic Orchestra. He was directing the music of Gustav Mahler, his acknowledged favorite composer. It was clear that agitation was mounting on his face as the music was being played, and finally he threw up his hands and let his mop of white hair stand on end as he expressed his frustration with the rendition of the orchestra. His words went something like this: "You are playing correct notes and are technically accurate, but *is it in you* to be vessels of the spirit of this great man? Because *if you can't* this music will be lost for all future generations. We owe it to this genius to share his spirit, and no one else will know what he gave us if we don't communicate it. So let us try to *get it ourselves* so we can pass it on."

Since watching that scene, I have thought about that image a lot—the passion of one great man to share, in truth, the greatness of another. I think this is what we have been called to do in this bicentennial year—to share our heritage and thus to be *vessels of the spirit* of the great women of the Society of the Sacred Heart.

I am privileged to try to capture the spirit of Philippine Duchesne so that the spirit of the woman is alive and so that others may know the substance of the woman who brought the Society of the Sacred Heart to this country.

What do we have in order to be vessels of her spirit?

We have her letters.

We have her accomplishments as they have borne fruit over time.

And we have the oral tradition about Philippine.

The Oral Tradition about Philippine

I have always been glad that I heard the stories of the woman before I read things she wrote or things written about her, because the oral tradition, for me, so formed me in admiration of her valiant spirit that they gave nuance to what I later read in her writings.

So let me back up to how I came to know Philippine. I am a graduate of Duchesne College in Omaha. After the noviceship, I returned to this institution until I went to Rome for final vows. Then I returned again as treasurer—so I had a long stint connected with this first institution in the Society to bear her name. And the religious who taught me there were imbued with the spirit of Philippine—they, too, had learned the stories well.

I think one of the reasons that Philippine was known so well in this Midwestern city was that another Sacred Heart convent was only three hours away by train, in Saint Joseph, Missouri. Many of the nuns who taught at Duchesne College were from Saint Joseph, and there is a direct line to Philippine through that institution. The school in Saint Joseph was founded in 1853; Philippine died in Saint Charles, Missouri, in 1852; the religious who were first sent to Saint Joseph knew Philippine personally, and so the oral tradition began authentically from the stories they told.

I remember so well hearing the stories as a college student, and then later as a nun, from the religious who would travel to Omaha for doctors or business appointments; and because I have always been fascinated by the pioneer experience, I would get them to tell me the stories. You see, my own family on my mother's side traveled the Oregon Trail and homesteaded on the West Coast. So pioneer stories are part of my own family history, and it was so much fun for me to understand that this great woman who brought the Society to the United States helped these pioneers along their way.

There was another period of time when I learned things about this woman that I had not known. The date was 1987; it was the year that we heard that Philippine Duchesne would be canonized. I was a member of the provincial team, and as word spread of this event in the life of the Church and in the life of our congregation, we began to receive correspondence that was truly amazing.

First, archivists from western states began contacting us about rivers, mountains, villages, and post offices that bore her name. Then, we received poetry and photographs of the etched windows at the University of Kansas from Beverly Boyd. And there was the day we received a call from the Potawatomi Indian Chief in Mound City, Kansas, asking what part the tribe would have to play in her canonization. Now, we did not initiate her canonization, and we had no idea what part anyone was to have in its celebration; but we did know that expectations were growing about this event from sources previously unknown to us.

We were learning about the impact of this woman from people who had not read her letters and who knew little about her experience or the experience of others within the Society. What these people knew was the impact of a holy woman who had so influenced them that they named rivers and lakes and towns for her and told her story so that it got handed down to the people who told it to us.

Then, in the spring of 1987, before the canonization, fifth and sixth generation nephews came to Saint Louis on pilgrimage in memory of their Great Aunt Philippine. They stayed at the cottage at Villa Duchesne and toured Saint Charles, Saint Ferdinand, and walked in Philippine's footsteps. They came to the provincial house and heard that I would be going to France in the late spring prior to the canonization and the General Chapter of 1988. They invited me to their home and wanted to accompany me to Grenoble. In Grenoble, they were able to garner an invitation to the apartment that was the actual living quarters of the Duchesne family. What a privilege it was for me to sit in the parlor of the Duchesne house and to see the very rooms in which she grew up.

As I looked around during the "high tea" in the Duchesne parlor, I saw a narrow door that looked something like a broom closet. It was my intuition that it could be the door that I had read about in some of the books on Philippine, the one that connected with the apartment of the Perier cousins. I asked in my very best French if I could open that door. The response was "Of course you can—but it opens only onto the porch that joins the next apartment." I remember my joy when I knew my intuition was right: this was the very door that Philippine and her cousins connected with in the dead of night when their respective parents were asleep! This was one of the stories I had heard about Philippine that I read later one of her biographies.

What did she do here?

Philippine has been *deemed a saint*; so we must pay attention to the reality, to what she accomplished. It seems extraordinary to me that one week after settling in Saint Charles, she opened the first free school west of the Mississippi. And the log states that "after a few more weeks," she opened two more schools. The journal continues, "There were twenty in the day school and the boarding school opened as well." In only three years she sent religious to Louisiana where more schools were opened. At her death nineteen schools had been founded in the United States and Canada, and the Religious of the Sacred Heart numbered 227. It seems to me that her pioneering spirit planted and cultivated the Society well in the New World.

Let us reflect on this reality. I see two conflicting realities in her. On the one hand, she was a woman of financial realism; and on the other hand, she was attempting to serve all of God's people—hence the several types of schools that she insisted on establishing. She was conflicted about good administration on the one hand and response to need on the other. And she was preoccupied about her personal success or failure; she talked about that in her letters, so obviously that was a part of what she struggled with in her own spiritual life.

What have we learned from her?

We have learned how to stay with something: she came, she stayed, and she kept us connected to the Center. She taught us about friendship beginning with her fifty years of friendship with Sophie Barat. She kept our spirit focused on all of God's people. She taught us about having "guts," or perhaps a nicer word is fortitude. She entered a convent, which she saw closed, returned home and moved to an apartment with a friend, and eventually got her convent back and saw it dissolved again; but she never lost her vision. If one thing didn't work, she let it develop into something else.

And what has been the fruit of her labor? Look at the students of the United States mission. There have been senators, mayors, editors, newscasters, actors, lawyers, presidents of corporations. Our students have mothered a United States president, founded schools, and opened an immigration agency. And some have gone to jail for causes they supported; the list could go on and on.

We have religious who have gone to Haiti, struggling to learn Creole just as Philippine struggled to learn English and the language of the Potawatomi tribe. All of this has taught us that this paradox of success and failure is only an apparent contradiction.

So going back to Leonard Bernstein's challenge to the New York Philharmonic Orchestra—let us give thanks for Philippine Duchesne's ability to be a vessel of the spirit of the Society. She convinced Sophie Barat to let her come; she had the staying power needed on the difficult frontier of our country, and she got this province of ours off and running. So just as Bernstein challenged his orchestra, let us who have learned from Philippine challenge one another to be good vessels of her spirit.

And further, may each of us strive to live deeply the values we embrace. Whether they are values we learned from our families, or in the work we have undertaken, or simply from our life experience, what is important is that we live what we believe.

The Frontier Further On

Margie Conroy, RSCJ

I ENTERED THE SOCIETY of the Sacred Heart in Albany, New York, for November 17th, then the feast of Blessed Philippine, many, many years ago. I left Montreal alone (by my own choice), seen off at the train station by my family and friends. I reached Albany in the afternoon and took a taxi to Kenwood. It was a dark, gloomy day, cold and damp and windy. When we reached Kenwood, I was amazed at the trees, so many of them, all completely bare, their branches moving in the wind. There were still some remnants of withered leaves, and a line from Hopkins came to my mind: "Margaret, are you grieving over goldengrove unleaving?"

Indeed, I was grieving as I approached this frontier into religious life that I was about to pass. It struck me how appropriate the trees and the time of the year were to Philippine Duchesne: Duchesne, born of oak, austere, hard wood.

Teilhard de Chardin says at the end of *The Phenomenon of Man* that all matter is striving towards consciousness, awareness. When I see trees dancing and bowing in the wind I believe it. I can sense them praising and thanking the God who created them, saying "Yes" to the stripping of their golden leaves and to the cold rain that darkened their bare branches, as life sank down into their roots until the frontier time of spring. And so it was with Philippine Duchesne, Philippine of Oak.

Philippine spent her life journeying to reach frontiers of one kind or another. At the age of twelve she decided to be a Visitation nun. At seventeen she knew the time had come. She walked up the mountain to Sainte-Marie d'En-Haut with her unsuspecting aunt and refused to leave.

But another frontier, much more painful, had to be crossed when she was twenty-two. The nuns were driven out of their convent by the Revolution. Then her life became one of risk and hard work, toiling up the mountain every day to minister to priests in the prison that Sainte-Marie had become, priests who were in danger of death.

After four years she crossed a new frontier, going back alone to Sainte-Marie, cleaning and repairing it, trying without success to bring back the nuns. A hard winter of seemingly endless years followed. Then Sophie Barat came like a long-awaited spring. Philippine blossomed and grew under her loving care that bore fruits of deep prayer and generosity. The Abbot of La Trappe, who had visited Missouri, rekindled in her heart the flame of longing for the missions she had felt as a child; and when Bishop Dubourg of Louisiana visited, it became an unquenchable fire. Sophie was conquered by Philippine's importunity and blessed and supported her mission.

So the next frontier Philippine crossed was the Atlantic, into a world she had never known, with a language she never managed to learn, into a culture she often found incomprehensible in spite of her generous efforts to adapt. Instead of the Indian children she had come for, she found herself caring for the daughters of the successful settlers in boarding schools. She felt herself to be a failure but clung to God in prayer for twenty years of loneliness and frustration.

Then, when she was seventy-two, came a new frontier, a new call to risk, a new spring. Father Verhaegen, SJ, asked that she be one of the group going to Sugar Creek in Kansas to minister to the Potawatomi Indian tribe. She went joyfully and continued her work of unremitting prayer, bringing forth sweet blossoms and fruits of holiness—"the woman who prays always," the Potawatomi called her.

After a year she was called back to Saint Louis to begin a long, final journey of patient, uncomplaining preparation for the final frontier, the call to eternal life. And there in heaven, she continues to flower and bring forth fruit without fail, her roots fed by the water that flows from the sanctuary of God's Heart. She intercedes for all the broken tribes of the world.

Philippine never saw France again after 1818. She is not a saint for the faint-hearted. She knew that the frontier was always farther on, requiring painful departures and often hard landings. We can ask her, because she is our own, to help us live outside our comfort zone in a risky, lonely, often incomprehensible era. If we do, then suddenly our branches will turn green, burst into bud, and flower, and we will dance for joy.

A Spirit of Innovation

Mary Moeschler[2]

ON NOVEMBER 17, 1985, Jeannette Kimball, RSCJ, directed a prayer service for the middle school students and faculty [at Forest Ridge] to celebrate Philippine Duchesne's feast. Sister Kimball, master teacher and lover of Philippine, sketched Rose Philippine Duchesne's life for us and planted a seed in my soul that has led me on a very personal journey to discover who this remarkable woman was and what she might say to Sacred Heart educators today.

As we prepare for her canonization in Rome on July 3, 1988, a brief overview of her life seems appropriate. Rose Philippine Duchesne was born into a wealthy and political family on August 29, 1769, in Grenoble, France. Much against her parents' wishes, she decided she wanted to become a religious, and at eighteen, she entered the Visitation convent. She was forced to leave as a result of the French Revolution. After eleven years of teaching religion to poor children, risking her life to bring good medicine and news to cholera victims in prison, feeding the hungry, and dressing the dead for burial, she met Madeleine Sophie Barat and joined the Society of the Sacred Heart, in 1804, just four years after Madeleine Sophie had founded her order dedicated to the education of young people. Philippine had a great desire to come to America and teach Native Americans, but it was not until 1818, after fourteen years of praying, begging, and laboring, that her dear friend Madeleine Sophie agreed to let her go.

So in March of 1818, at the age of forty-eight, Philippine and four companions sailed for the New World in the *Rebecca*. When Philippine left France, she knew that she would never see her family or friends again. She was a risk-taker and totally confident that God would take care of her! After a two-month voyage marked by storms and illness, the little group arrived in New Orleans. Several months later, Philippine proceeded upriver to establish the first free school for girls west of the Mississippi River in Saint Charles, Missouri. Her

---

2 The author was director of the middle school at Forest Ridge, served on the faculty from 1971, and served for several years on the School Committee of the Network of Sacred Heart Schools.

heroic example in gladly bearing privations of every kind—lack of food and water, intense cold and no fuel, inadequacy of books and classroom materials—is a courageous model for those of us who think we have inadequate resources today.

After twenty-three years of establishing and nurturing Sacred Heart schools for the children of settlers, she was finally sent to the Potawatomi Indians in Sugar Creek, Kansas. Even this led, not to the realization of her dream, but to further disappointment. Unable to learn their language, she was accepted with kindness by the Native People. Her declining health resulted in her being sent back to Saint Charles, where she died, in 1852, at the age of eighty-three. To the end, Philippine saw herself as an inadequate superior and as a failure as a missionary.

Simply facing daily hardships, suffering, sorrow, and failure does not make one a candidate for formal canonization, so why is Philippine being canonized? Look at her legacy. She is the person who brought the Society of the Sacred Heart to the United States. One hundred seventy years ago she opened her first school. Today, Forest Ridge is one of twenty-two Sacred Heart schools and colleges that span this country. Her prayer, her perseverance, and her faithfulness to a vision she loved, enabled her to overcome the obstacles of loneliness and disconnectedness from family and friends. Her commitment to being among people as a servant urges each of us to reexamine our vocations on a daily basis.

Saints are canonized because they are models for us. By acknowledging saints, the Church reminds us that they are still with us and that their spirit can still inspire us. Three official miracles are required for a canonization. The three miracles attributed to Philippine occurred on behalf of two Religious of the Sacred Heart and a friend of the Society's house at Ponce in Puerto Rico.

There is no doubt in my mind that Philippine still speaks to us today. To adults, perhaps she is saying "Hang on . . . believe in taking risks." To those who are feeling old, her journey to a new land and a strange people shows us that at all stages of life we can embrace new experiences and share the gifts of the Sacred Heart. In spite of illness, broken relationships, misunderstandings, or uniquely personally human challenges, there is meaning in whatever we are experiencing. She encourages us to be faithful, to persevere, to have a sense of purpose, and to be confident that our lives are meaningful. To students and young people, she may be saying "Leave the familiar for the unfamiliar. Reflect on those things that you want to pack in your heart for life—what dreams you want to hang onto—what goals you have set for yourself—what experiences you want to carry deep inside you—what inner strength you will need to nurture you into adulthood." She demands of all of us that we learn to wait. How trying that is in this automated world of ours!

Today, the complexion of Sacred Heart education is changing across America. With the decrease in the number of religious, lay people have begun to take a more active role in carrying on the work of the Society. It is my belief that the graces from the canonization will inspire innovative ways of lay/religious collaboration leading to a new expression of Sacred Heart education.

Philippine lived during a tumultuous time in history; so do we. If we can internalize her spirit—if we live as she lived—in faith, in hope, and in love, then we, too, can make a difference in our world.

To Philippine Duchesne (Linn County, Kansas, 1841)

Beverly Boyd

What were you doing here, old woman,
old woman from France,
out here among the Indians,
the Osage and the Potawatomi,
with their strange languages,
and their ghost dance?

This is the great spirit's country,
and neither theirs nor yours
willed her by other forces,
governments, agreements, treaties, wars.
Over the ocean and the Missouri,
and in a wooden cart
crossing the Kansas tallgrass
with only God in your heart:
what were you thinking of, old woman,
with your old woman's lines and pains,
out here among the Indians
in the Kansas winds and rains?

I know you well, old woman;
I know what was in your heart
riding back east for Saint Louis
the way you came here, in a cart,
and back down the Missouri River,
you had come so far,
nothing to show for the hardship,
the work of God your last star.

Now by the Mississippi buried,
old woman from sweet France,
the Indians here still recall you,
though some keep the old customs
and their ghost dance.
You are "The Woman Who Prays Always"
in the legend of their past;
there is a shrine no one visits
where the winds and land are vast.

Philippine Duchesne: The First Missionary of the Heart[3]

Jane Cannon

FOR PHILIPPINE, THE PROSPECT of coming to America was the fulfillment of a forty-year-old dream—and a dream laced with constant badgering (if you will) to remind her superior of her fondest hope. She was a woman who, in the words of her biographer, Louise Callan, RSCJ, "broke a trail that has led thousands of souls to Christ and has broadened into a highway of culture in the United States, Canada and Latin America."

Throughout the early years, committed to the community's mission, Philippine never forsook the goal that she had adopted during her childhood conversations with the missionary priests. And so she was understandably hopeful when Bishop William Dubourg visited the convent in Paris in 1817 to ask Mother Barat for Religious of the Sacred Heart to come and work in his new diocese, which basically comprised the whole Louisiana Territory. His Indian stories fired anew the old dream that *both* nuns shared. And all the while Sophie was thinking, "Things are certainly looking good for Philippine now!" But although she would have liked to give the good bishop some missionaries for this holy endeavor, Father Varin advised her not to, and so she told the bishop that her order was still too new to be able to spare a group yet. He was about to leave when Philippine burst into the room, threw herself on the floor and begged, "Your consent, Mother, give your consent!" Sophie did give her consent—as we all know—and the rest (as they say) is history. The next year was spent making preparations for the journey and choosing the nuns who would be Philippine's companions as the first missionaries of the Heart. They tried as well as they could to imagine what they would need for their new life on the American frontier and—for that matter—what Sophie could afford to provide for them.

Much later in her life, during her ministry in Saint Louis, it was not unusual for the priests to visit and tell Philippine about their adventures with the Indians. Father Peter De Smet, the well-known Jesuit missionary who had traveled as far as the Pacific, always visited Philippine when he was in Saint Louis. He wrote later of her: "I never returned from one

---

3 Excerpts from a talk given to the AASH, Los Angeles.

of these visits but with an increase of edification, with a full conviction that I had conversed with a truly living saint. I always considered Mother Duchesne as the greatest protector of our Indian missions." Father Hoecken, another Jesuit, was able to speak fifteen different Indian dialects—a skill that Philippine would come to envy with all her heart.

But it was Father Verhaegen, who came to visit at City House that day to discuss the plans for the upcoming trip to Sugar Creek. As was always the custom, out of courtesy Mother Duchesne (now an old lady of seventy-two) was included in the conversation in the parlor. She had sensed in the preceding weeks that this mission was in the works, but the nuns had tried to spare her the heartbreak of hearing the plans, since, obviously, she was unfit for the trip. As the conversation with the young Jesuit progressed, tears rolled down the cheeks of the old woman bowed over in the corner. Finally Father Verhaegen sensed what the nuns had neglected to mention; and he blurted out: "What? Well, surely she is coming too! She, above all, must go! Why, even if she can use only one leg, she will come! Why, if we have to carry her all the way on our shoulders, she is coming with us. She may not be able to do much work, but she will assure success to this mission by praying for us. Her very presence will draw down all manner of heavenly favors on the work."

So the die was cast. Philippine Duchesne was finally to realize her lifelong dream! Her health seemed to improve immediately as she and the other nuns organized their supplies for the journey, which would take them by steamboat (four days) up the Missouri River to Westport (now part of Kansas City) then inland by oxcart for eight more days. The Potawatomi, among whom they would be living, had a heartbreaking history of migration across the country, precipitated by the government, whose history of moving Indian tribes is notorious. Starting in Wisconsin, they were transplanted to Indiana and then force-marched in what was called the "Trail of Death" to their new location in Kansas. Before Philippine lived with them they had negotiated no fewer than thirty-nine treaties with the white man and his government—and always managed to get the short end of the stick.

But the day of their arrival in Sugar Creek was a glorious day in Philippine's life. This tribe of Indians was peaceful and had begged the Jesuits to bring them priests or nuns who would live among them and tell them about God. The parade of braves that rode out from the village to greet the exhausted party of blackrobes performed precision exercises on horseback and certainly conveyed the welcome that made Philippine's seventy-two years of waiting all worthwhile.

Once they arrived at the Indian village the nuns were disappointed to discover that the home they had been promised was not built yet. And so from July to October they lived in a small hut that belonged to one of the Indians. They opened their school immediately and had fifty young girls who came for instruction plus older women who learned to sew, wash clothes and to sweep. We all know the sad burden of the language barrier that had crippled Philippine even in her efforts to converse in English; so, of course, this Potawatomi tongue was even more impossible for her. But she was a good needlewoman all her life, so surely she could teach a little simply by demonstration.

Philippine's first letter to Madeleine Sophie Barat from Sugar Creek opened with these jubilant words: "At last we have reached the country of our desires! There are no difficulties here except when people worry too much about tomorrow." The nuns were fascinated by the way of life of the Indians—and impressed by their goodness. Even though Philippine had little conversation with them, the Potawatomi loved her. Mother Lucille Mathevon, who was in charge of this mission, reported, "They bring the 'good old lady' all manner of things—fresh corn, newly laid eggs, chickens, wild plums, and sweet, clean straw for her pallet." Their experience with her was based, as much on what they saw (a figure of pure holiness) as on what they might hear from her lips. We all know the story of how she was "tested" by the little children who couldn't believe that someone so old had the physical discipline—let alone sublime mystical union with her "Great Spirit"—that enabled her to stay for so many hours in prayer. When their new house was in the final stages of its construction, the nuns would encourage her to go to the little log chapel to stay out of harm's way. You can imagine how happy she was to comply with this urging! So she would trudge across the snow and remain there for long, cold hours talking to her God. As she knelt there, motionless for so long, the Indians would steal in and watch her intently, then noiselessly approach her and kiss the hem of her worn habit or the fringe of her old shawl. *Qua-kah-ka-num-ad* they would call her (Woman Who Prays Always).

Mother Barat also sent Mother Galitzine to investigate the situation in the Potawatomi Mission. Lucille Mathevon—as much as she loved Philippine (revered her even!)—feared for her life on this rough prairie frontier. Mother Galitzine was deeply moved by the piety of the Indians (as were the other nuns) but agreed that this was no place for a woman as old and broken as Philippine Duchesne.

Mother Mathevon had already written her concerns: "She is here just to suffer, for she has aged much in this short time and is sometimes like a little child. She no longer has the fine mind of other days. She is feeble, her limbs are swollen; her digestion is poor. I fear she will have a stroke. To tell you the truth, we cannot understand how Father Verhaegen could have insisted on bringing her here. But he said that she would pray for the missions, and she must be given the consolation of dying here. All she can do at present is pray, sometimes lying for a little while on her bed, and knit stockings. That is all. It is a great anxiety for us. We are doing all we can for her. She has done so much for the Society. It is only right that we give her all possible care in her old age."

Philippine, on the other hand, would have welcomed death there in the place she had begun to think she would never reach. She herself wrote to Sophie: "They tell us that there are many saints buried in the little Indian cemetery. When I walk alone out of doors, I always go there and I kneel and beg of God the favor of being buried beside them." Bishop Kenrick, the new bishop of Saint Louis, agreed with Mothers Mathevon and Galitzine; and so, after just one year among her beloved Potawatomi, Philippine and Father Verhaegen made the hard, ten-day journey back to Saint Louis. After a brief stay at the City House, she moved to Saint Charles. Of this decision she said: "God knows the reason for the recall. That is enough."

And haven't we known other nuns who have also bowed to this higher power? Philippine's devotion to the Society was greater than any other force in her life. She showed that as she came back to a hidden life in Saint Charles, where she lived for ten more years. As long as she was able, the nuns gave her tasks that would make her feel useful in the life of the school. There were always a few French speaking children—even then—and these she taught catechism in a little room in the basement of the brick convent. She would take her place in her classroom early so that she would not have to disturb the mother whose room she had to walk through to get to hers.

Somewhere on our campus in Saint Charles there was, for many years, a pear tree that Mother Duchesne had grafted. She was very fond of it and, in her old age, liked to sit under it and pray. Often she was seen there crying—presumably for the many ways that she believed she had failed in her mission. One of her joys, during these last years of her life, was the occasional visit from Father De Smet, who always stopped to see her and report on his Indian missions when he was in the area. He said of her after her death: "She has sown deep roots in American soil, and one day they will reap an abundant harvest."

One of Philippine's great sorrows during these last years of her life was a cessation of communication with Mother Barat. This seems a mystery to many, and some conjecture points out several possible reasons for the heartbreaking void that left this poor old woman bereft of contact for *four years*! Sophie Barat was, by then, mother general of more than 2,000 religious, so she was obviously very busy. Maybe some letters were even lost. Additionally, a directive had gone out to all the nuns to write to the superior general only when necessary. In 1847, Sophie *did* write a letter to Philippine and sent it to be delivered by Amélie Jouve (Philippine's niece and a Religious of the Sacred Heart). Amélie had just been appointed to a new mission in Canada; but, since Sophie had not heard from Philippine in a long time, she decided to send Amélie via a little detour through Saint Charles. When Amélie handed her the letter from Sophie, Philippine said, "So our mother general still thinks of me? Still loves me? She has been so good as to show me that love by sending you to visit me?" In her reply (which she surely began to write that very day), she wrote to Sophie: "I was sorrowfully convinced that I had lost my place in your heart; and, because I thought it was through some fault of mine, my own heart was the more grief stricken."

This pen portrait by Mother Jouve gives us a poignant picture of her aunt: "Among the many virtues that were noticeable in Mother Duchesne, these were the most prominent: her devotion to the Sacred Heart in the Blessed Sacrament, her love of poverty, her deep humility, her self-denial and penance, her zeal for the salvation of souls, and her charity. She was of a naturally serious disposition, yet was always joyous and animated at the community recreations or when religious came for visits in her room. By reason of her natural disposition toward self-contempt and an exaggerated notion of personal responsibility for all that went amiss around her, *she was her own heaviest cross*. She misplaced things she needed, forgot things she had promised to do, spoke hastily at times. But never did she allow such faults to pass without reparation."

Two days before her death—on November 18, 1852—Philippine Duchesne had another important visitor. Mother Anna du Rousier, who had been dispatched by the mother general to go to South America, was directed to travel by way of Saint Charles to deliver a message to Mother Duchesne. This was the same Anna du Rousier who, as a little girl, had met Philippine Duchesne when she and her missionary band stopped in Poitiers on their way to Bordeaux to board the *Rebecca* for America. Anna had thrilled at that moment to the missionary zeal that was contagious and permanently stamped on her heart. Once in the room with the saintly old nun and having delivered the blessing of the mother general, Mother du Rousier asked Philippine for *her* blessing. Obligingly the old lady traced a Cross on the younger nun's forehead. For years afterwards Anna du Rousier said, "I still seem to feel that cross."

We can only imagine the spirit of prayer that permeated the house in Saint Charles on the morning of November 18 as the nuns anticipated the imminent death of their dear Mother Duchesne. One little sister who was concerned about her comfort hurried in to light a little fire in the brazier in her room and was—typically—scolded for such a frivolous waste and received the suggestion that it would serve the dying nun better if she said an *Ave* for her. When the nun replied that the whole community was in the chapel adjacent to her cell praying for her, Philippine sighed, "Oh, how fortunate I am to die in a house where charity dwells."

The pastor at the neighboring Saint Charles Borromeo Church, Father Verhaegen (the dear Jesuit who had insisted on taking Philippine to Kansas—and the one who sadly brought her back a year later) was the one who brought her Communion on that last day—and then remained with her until the Angelus struck at noon and her eighty-two-year old body gave up its spirit.

Sometimes people who come to Saint Charles on tours (and I have to tell you that almost all of them are either senior citizen or school groups) ask us if Philippine Duchesne is the patron saint of anything in particular. And, while we have to admit that nothing has been officially proclaimed in that area, we sometimes suggest that she could be considered a patron of senior citizens. Certainly she knew the trials and tribulations that the elderly suffer. Do these quotes strike a familiar chord with any of you who, like me, sometimes catch ourselves wondering what the not-too-distant future holds: "I feel that I am a worn out instrument, a useless walking stick that is fit only to be hidden in a dark corner. God allows everything to deepen this impression in my soul." Or this one that teeters on the positive/negative scale: "I am really healthier than I like. During recent years I have often thought I should die soon. Now I fear I shall live to be a hundred—as there is no prospect of death in the near future. I am troubled at the prospect of the infirmities and uselessness of old age. However, I am not there yet. The lack of servants leaves me with plenty to do!"

I think sometimes we may be surprised by Philippine's depression—just as we were when we heard, not too long ago, that Blessed Mother Teresa of Calcutta suffered great doubts during her holy life. But no! These were women of intense faith and incredible love, who just held the bar very high for themselves.

I chose as my title for this talk today, "Philippine Duchesne, First Missionary of the Heart." And that is true. She was the first missionary of the Society of the Sacred Heart. But she certainly wasn't the last. Many of the religious whom she trained went on to spread the Society to other parts of the world, and it's still happening today! And this work is not reserved for Religious! Last year at our school in Saint Charles, we focused our year on the life and vision of Janet Erskine Stuart. This quote jumped out at me then and reinforced—at least 100 years after her vision for her "little Society"—what Saint Madeleine Sophie had dreamed for us: "We must remember that each one of our children is destined for a mission in life. Neither we nor they can know what it is, but we must know and make them believe that each one has a mission in life and that she is bound to find out what it is, that there is some special work for God that will remain undone unless she does it, some place in life that no one else can fill."

Remember this patron saint of senior citizens who didn't dream of huge achievements but asked only to do the work that God held out to her. She said: "We cultivate a very small field for Christ but we love it, knowing that God does not require great achievements but a heart that holds nothing back for self."

On the wall of one of our parlors in Saint Charles there is a quote by T. Gavan Duffy about Mother Duchesne. Here is what that priest had to say: "What have we learned from her? The value of a steadfast purpose, the success of failure, and the unimportance of our standards of success; the power of grace released by deep, divine desires and simple duties daily done."

Testimony of Father De Smet, SJ

Missionary to the Native Americans
Friend of Philippine

ONE OF THOSE WHO listened to Father De Smet speak of Mother Duchesne in 1847 made these notes of what he said:

"He said she had climbed all the rungs of the ladder of sanctity, and never had he seen a soul more ardent in love for Our Lord. In his opinion, she rivaled Saint Teresa. Never had he known a person who was poorer in all that concerned her private life, and in this she imitated Saint Francis of Assisi. Nor a more apostolic soul, eager for the salvation of souls, and he thought Saint Francis Xavier had shared with her his zeal for the conversion of the infidels. Ending his talk he said: Now she is on the sorrowful way of Calvary to which old age and infirmities have condemned her, but no matter how hard that road may seem to her, she is climbing it with all the fervor of youth. She has struck deep roots in American soil, and they will one day bear an abundant harvest. I should not be surprised if some day she were raised to our altars."

Twenty years after her death, Father De Smet wrote:

I keep the memory of Mère Duchesne in the highest respect and veneration. Her praise has been and is on the lips, not only of her own Sisters in religion, but of all those who had the honor and the happiness of her acquaintance. On every return from my Indian missionary visits, I deemed it a most agreeable duty to pay my respects to good Mother Duchesne, and I never returned from one of these visits but with an increase of edification, with a full conviction that I had conversed with a truly living saint. I always considered Mother Duchesne as the greatest protector of our Indian missions. For years she offered two Communions a week and daily prayers for the conversion of the Indians. She loved these poor, benighted children dearly and nothing seemed to make her happier than to hear of their conversions, of their fervor and zeal in the practice of their religious duties after having entered the true fold of our Divine Redeemer. I can entertain, no doubt, many were brought over to the Holy Faith of Christ by the many acts of mortification she performed, and by the constant prayers she offered up for the salvation of these, her dearly beloved Indian children ...

(Callan, *Philippine Duchesne*, pp. 686-687; abridged edition, pp. 462-463.)

Friendship of Two Saints

The Austere Beauty of Sanctity

Gertrude Bodkin, RSCJ
Extract from a Conference to Religious of the Sacred Heart
February 7, 1935

WE HAVE A PAINTING of our Mother Foundress before us, and the more we study her the more we see how lovable the picture is; how free, how wise, how whole her life was. What is it that is so attractive? We do not know. It is very hard to put one's finger on it. One could almost say it was a glowing Christianity, a likeness to Christ, a something of his spirit and of his Heart and of his love translated into a human life, into our life. This is extremely appealing to us because of its beauty, because of its wholeness, because of its sanity, because of its humanness. There is nothing ultra or exaggerated, nothing hard or rough. All seems so natural. What is it? Just what it should be, just what we would have expected Our Lord to be, or his mother, and our hearts go out irresistibly to that.

Saint Madeleine Sophie expressed the spirit of the Society, our way of life in its perfection. It is what we all want to aim at and to be; it is what we could very easily live with our whole heart and would. It is what we are to practice year after year with untiring perseverance because we have seen something in it that has won our mind and heart. When we understand that, we see that it is easy enough to love the Society and everything connected with it, as well as every means that allows the Society to fulfill its mission.

In Mother Duchesne there is another picture, quite a different kind of beauty. It is an austere beauty, a beauty of line rather than color. It is something stern but of great beauty all the same. It has not the glow but it has the form and lines of the portrait of our Mother Foundress. It shows us the Society as represented in a different temperament, in different surroundings, in a different character—beautiful in its own way. It is whole-hearted, vigorous, intense, appealing to those who love something heroic and strong. It is not for everybody, but nobody could remain unimpressed by it. From what source did Mother Duchesne draw her love of the Society? There is nothing natural about it. Her first attraction was to the contemplative life. Yet when she met Saint Madeleine Sophie, her heart went out to the ideal that was presented to her—unlike anything she could have conceived of herself. She put her best qualities into the pursuit of that ideal; and although she may perhaps never have attained to the sweetness and the human charm of Saint Madeleine Sophie, she left her mark on the Society. Looking at those two women is like seeing a study of the same object done in two different media.

In Mother Duchesne's life we see all the hard lines, all the straight lines, the skeleton on which the anatomy or figure was built—beautiful in its straightness, symmetry, unity, but without the glow and the radiant charm. Under Mother Barat's sweetness and wisdom, there are all the strong lines that stood out so patently in Mother Duchesne. They are all there, but there is something more. They are covered over, as it were, so that the stark lines would not be startling or repugnant to weak souls. Our Lord did for Saint Madeleine Sophie something of what he did for his mother, clothing her with gentleness, meekness, and tenderness. Just as he himself could not convey to us in human form all he had to give us but had to have his mother as a complement to fill out all the sweetness, mercy, and goodness of his life, so the Society had to give us two great saints to complete the picture of our vocation.

It seems that the Church may soon pronounce upon the sanctity of Philippine Duchesne and give her to us as a model, and when the Church does this we can be infallibly sure that she is an example of the vocation God has given us. We must try in our small way to be worthy of these great saints by following in their footsteps. We know how to venerate and please Mother Duchesne; it would be by fidelity to the Constitutions—*our* fidelity to *our* Constitutions. Each one is faithful in a slightly different way, because each one's conscience and mental conception are somewhat different according to the temperament of the person. The Constitutions are catholic; they suit many minds and hearts. Women of quite opposite characteristics have equally shown forth the love of Christ in living according to them. We can lean to one side or the other according to our attraction or temperament, but the essentials of both we must all have. We know well enough the essentials of Mother Duchesne's life: her austerity, her self-sacrifice, her zeal carried to the point of self-immolation, the generosity that accepted everything that came her way for the love of souls and the love of the Heart of Jesus.

What came her way? Humiliation, contempt, failure, hiddenness. Remember, the last ten years of her life were spent in obscurity. She not only accepted that; she loved it. It was what she wanted and prayed for. She took it with her whole heart. She was pleased with it. She never pitied herself. What did pain her was the thought that she might have disappointed our Mother Foundress, that she might have contributed to failure by her own imperfection. That, I think, preyed a little on her mind and heart, for she was not gifted with that assurance that God sometimes gives to childlike hearts. She searched her heart as the saints of old did and reproached herself. She suffered from that, but never from the fact that she was humbled or hidden or put aside or made of little account—that she rejoiced in.

We have many opportunities for rejoicing ourselves in little hidden things, and we often spoil them by pitying ourselves, by looking on them as injuries, by becoming a little bitter. There is nothing bitter in these events when we accept them as our daily bread, which God has provided. If God has given them, what can be wrong with them? They must be steps on our road to sanctity. If we are really in earnest and want to be whole-hearted with God, we must accept them as such, refusing to look at secondary causes. Who said a thing or who did it—what does it matter? This is something that God has provided for me that I may give him my whole self, my whole heart. I receive it and thank God for it whole-heartedly. Anyone who sees that attitude as beautiful, noble, sublime knows that it will attract others.

We are now reaping the fruit of Mother Duchesne's sanctity; the success of our apostolate is the fruit of her zeal. In thanksgiving she asks us to consider her way of life, to appreciate it a little more, not to be too much afraid to try it in any way we like, in a small way perhaps, but to give it a trial—to try to love the things she loved. I think she will help us mightily to love them. If we should come to love the things she loved—poverty, humility, abnegation, and readiness to give everything in zeal—I think our road to sanctity would be a short one and our success in the Society would be perfect.

A Sustaining Friendship

Margaret Williams, RSCJ
November 21, 1986

AT THE HEART OF the Christian mystery lies the further mystery of interpersonal rela-tionship. Its archetype is the inner life of the Trinity, of the three Persons in one God, and it is reflected in the Communion of Saints. This awesome mystery has an endearing human name; we call it friendship. The Constitutions of the Society of the Sacred Heart assure us: "Friendship is a priceless and demanding gift, which may be given to us along the way of love and of faith. It will be all the truer in the measure in which it opens us more fully to the mission. At the same time, it recalls God's faithful love. Our union with Jesus will give transparency and joy to our friendships."

Madeleine Sophie Barat had a genius for friendship and said of it: "This, we must recog-nize, is true friendship, to forget ourselves," while of herself she said: "The only good quality recognizable in me is the constancy of my affections." She called her friends "those with whom I feel at ease," and dearest among them all was Philippine Duchesne.

The friendship between these two was forged at Grenoble in 1804 when the impetuous Philippine threw herself at the feet of Madeleine Sophie, exclaiming: "How beautiful on the mountains are the feet of those bringing peace." It deepened steadily until the death of Philippine in 1852. And yet, out of those forty-eight years, these friends spent only four and a half living together, two at Grenoble when Philippine was a novice, two and a half in Paris when she was already begging to go overseas. For the remaining forty-four years they were separated at first by short and then by vast distances.

Happily for us, each had a genius for letter-writing, and each kept the other's letters. Madeleine Sophie said: "Correspondence absorbs my time, but truly it is a chore that I love. Without this wonderful invention, how could we live far from those we hold dear?" Those letters that took so long to reach the heart-hungry recipients built an invisible suspen-sion bridge across the Atlantic Ocean. Over that bridge came the love and wisdom of our Foundress who entrusted the Society in the western hemisphere to Philippine and her dauntless companions. And so this incomparable friendship came to include us all.

— 50 —

From the first Madeleine Sophie realized that she could share all she had with Philippine. "I feel the need of pouring out my heart into that of a friend to whom our Lord seems to have given the same desire of making him known and loved." At this level friends may substitute for each other. "I have so great a desire that you should love Jesus that I don't even consider myself, because I want to pass into your soul the confidence and the love that I should have for him, so that you may love him for me." Still more, it is possible that one person may fulfill the uncompleted vocation of another. When Madeleine Sophie found herself, as she said, "nailed to France," she said: "Have I given up my desire for the foreign missions? It increases every day, and I have been asking that one of my companions should carry it out, and that the Holy Spirit himself should prepare and lead her." This companion was Philippine.

Yet these friends on fire with the same passionate dreams differed in temperament. Madeleine Sophie envied the rugged health that allowed Philippine to pray all night, and the courage that sent her headlong into the unknown. With patience she trained Philippine through twelve long years to bend her own impatient will to God's slow ways. Philippine's understanding of her call was according to the classic mission mandate: "Go forth, teach, baptize." Madeleine Sophie tempered this according to the charism of the Society: "Why can we not say to the universe, know his Heart?"

Madeleine Sophie was lonely after the sailing of the *Rebecca*: "Since coming to your dear mountain, how many memories both sweet and heart-breaking struggle with each other! How hard it was not only not to find you here but to know that you are so far away from me. Faith helps me, and forgetting myself I see that you are very happy!" But Philippine still needed help, and Madeleine Sophie wrote warningly: "Times change, and we must change with them and modify our views." "At this distance, how can I judge? Make your own decisions and tell me of them." Philippine had her dark hours: "I feel that I am an outworn instrument that is fit only to be hid in a corner. God allows everything to deepen this impression in my soul. I have never at any time attracted people's confidence, and the same is true here. We have been obliged to have our night recreations in the kitchen. So in the midst of noise and dishwashing, with the wind sweeping in on all sides, we renewed our sacrifice when we remembered the evenings in France." Madeleine Sophie sent her strong comfort: "Now there is only the cross and naked detachment. It must be that way. Adieu, dear mother and beloved daughter. I am losing my hope of ever seeing you again, Philippine."

It took twenty-one more years of waiting for Philippine to at last reach her Indians, where the children saw in her "the Woman who Prays Always," Qua-kah-ka-num-ad. She stayed with them for one brief year, with her face still turned to the horizon. Still she pleaded with Madeleine Sophie: "I feel now the same longings that I experienced in France when I first begged to come to America, the same longings I felt for the Indian missions once I reached this country. They say that in the Rocky Mountains people live to be one hundred years old. As my health has improved, and I am only seventy-three, I think I shall have at least ten more years to work. So will you not authorize me to go farther west if they want me to?"

Instead, Philippine was sent back to Saint Charles and spent ten years in waiting while letters from her best friend inexplicably stopped coming. When at last her niece, Amélie Jouve, came from France with healing assurances of love, Philippine wrote: "Your letter and your gifts, dear Mother, have been a life-giving balm to my soul." She died on November 18, 1852, having passed on her mission to Anna du Rousier who stood by her side in the name of Madeleine Sophie Barat. The latter wrote to Amélie: "You prayed for me to your holy aunt, I hope, when you visited her grave. The good master has given me no more than one of her virtue and capacity." Yet she still hoped, as the years went by that someone could still take Philippine's place. When a call came from the Far East in 1858, she said to the probanists: "A zealous missionary said to me lately: 'They are waiting for you in China.' Alas, I had to give up the thought and my heart is heavy, but subjects are lacking. . . . When there was question of America, I did not hesitate to send Mother Duchesne, for I knew that she was according to the heart of God, and now that the harvest is so great, can I find no one of whom the divine Master wills to make use to do great things?"

A Tiny Part of a Great Harvest

Kathleen Hughes, RSCJ
Saint Charles, November 18, 2008

WE'VE JUST HEARD A reading that could not be more perfectly suited to a celebration of Rose Philippine Duchesne: "... unless a grain of wheat falls into the ground and dies it remains a single grain, but if it dies it bears a rich harvest." We are, each one of us, some tiny part of the harvest that Philippine planted 190 years ago when she arrived on this soil of Saint Charles.

> We are a harvest
> planted by her extraordinary labors,
> watered with her sufferings and her tears,
> pruned by her courage and confidence,
> and cultivated faithfully and daily
> by her deep life of prayer and her longing for God.

It was just twenty years ago that the Church declared Philippine a saint. Unfortunately sometimes the word "saint" has a way of distancing us from those so named, but, in fact, Philippine was very much like us:
> She drove her family crazy.
> She was given to excesses.
> She loved deeply.
> She longed to make a difference in the world.
> She often doubted her own efforts.
> She experienced loneliness and frustration and failures of every kind.

Basically she stumbled towards holiness, loving God, and seeking God's will, and persevering despite incredible obstacles from without and lingering self-doubt from within.

Philippine was a woman with a global vision. Often she is pictured with a map of the world on her lap. She longed to be about mission, especially bringing God's love to the New World.

She was a woman on the margins who said once "I am always drawn to the most deprived." And she was drawn

to the destitute masses after the French Revolution

to the desperately ill on shipboard coming to the States

and to *every* social class once she reached these shores.

Her boarding schools supported her free schools and her work with orphans, and meanwhile, her desire to work with her beloved Potawatomi was postponed for years until her strength waned and her health had failed, and she could be simply a presence among them—and that, only for a year.

She was a woman of deep relationships

and she perfectly illustrates the importance of friendship in living a holy life,

whether in marriage, religious life, single life or priesthood,

whether in professional or ministerial commitments . . . friendship is critical.

Madeleine Sophie and Philippine were separated by an ocean for the last thirty-four years of Philippine's life, but the bond between them fueled both their lives, and incidentally it guaranteed that we would remain one international congregation and not become an independent American order. Their friendship demonstrates how deep and loving relationships help us stay honest before God, support our dreams and desires, challenge us to be our best self, knowing we are loved, and provide presence and words of tenderness and care in crisis. . . .

And crises aplenty Philippine had! She was a woman of disappointments, broken dreams, incredible suffering and weakness. . . . She suffered all the privations of frontier life, perhaps most of all because she could not spare her sisters the same hardships. She was never able to master the English or native languages. She saw houses and schools close and some of her first companions leave. She saw her sisters die in their prime from cholera and other diseases. She experienced painful misunderstandings as letters crossed the ocean, or were lost en route, and as her plans had to be cancelled or deferred.

And perhaps the greatest suffering of all, she considered herself always an incompetent leader for the community, and she begged again and again to be replaced.

She was, she thought, a failure, and yet her very weakness made her most like Christ, the perfect disciple, of whom it is said in the Epistle to the Hebrews:

"[H]e was able to minister to others because he himself was beset by weakness!"

Living as we do in a world little tolerant of failure, the life of Rose Philippine Duchesne has much to teach us about the grain of wheat that falls into the ground and dies and thus produces a rich harvest.

I sometimes wonder if Philippine had these very words in mind when she wrote:
We cultivate a very small field for Christ,
but we love it,
knowing that God does not require great achievements,
but a heart that holds back nothing for itself.

Perhaps as we turn to the table of the Eucharist we could ask for just such a heart.

The Friendship of Wisdom and Solitude

Rose Marie Quilter, RSCJ
July 1, 1987

ONCE UPON A TIME, long ago across the sea, there was a woman whose name was Wisdom. True to her name, she had grown wise beyond her years, for she had been born of Fire. Since she continually drew life from Fire, her face and her heart had a glow that warmed everyone who knew her.

One day, a friend came to Wisdom with a message. He told her that on a snow-capped mountaintop, many days journey away, at the far end of the kingdom, someone awaited her.

The people of the mountaintop held the Waiting One in scorn. They declared her to be very foolish—a dreamer of dreams. Odd. Everyone knew that she had squandered her family fortune to buy a drafty old mansion. She dreamt of rekindling a hearth there, but those who came to share her dream quickly left. The townsfolk whispered among themselves that the Dreamer deserved her fate. Who could live with her? They called her, "The Solitary One."

The Solitary One remained in the drafty old mansion, hoping against hope for the melting of the mountain snows and the coming of spring. One bitterly cold December afternoon, the Wind whistled through the long bare corridors of the old mansion on the mountain with a lonely sigh. The Solitary One sighed with it, "How long?" It had become a refrain for her. But she sang it bravely back to the Wind, and hoped against hope.

That very day, something wonderful happened. A carriage stopped in front of the mansion. The ancient door of oak resounded with a gentle but persistent knocking. The Solitary One opened the door, and a young woman crossed the threshold. She was slightly built, but full of life, with a glow about her, a quickness—like a cheerful fire, burning in the hearth. The Solitary One wept for joy. She fell at the feet of young Wisdom, and kissed them.

"How beautiful on the mountaintops are the feet of those who bring tidings of peace!" she exclaimed. Suddenly, though the Wind continued to blow through the old mansion, the place was filled with amber sunlight.

Years passed. The Solitary One, warmed by the same Fire as young Wisdom, began to grow wise herself. She continued to dream great dreams. Now that her mountaintop had become a glowing hearth once more, she dreamt of a people far across the sea, calling to her on the voice of the Wind. In fact, she dreamt of people all across the world, and night after night, she heard their cries.

Young Wisdom listened tenderly and often to Solitude's dream, for she shared it. She blessed the Dreamer, smiled tenderly, and said, "Not yet. When the time is right, we will know. We will see it in the Firelight. For now, you must wait."

So, once again, Solitude waited. She did not always wait patiently. But she cared for her dream right there at home. She was the first to arise in the morning, and the last to retire at night, and all day long she did her best to tend the Fire. But at night she was free. Her heart went on long journeys, and with the help of the Wind, she spread the Fire to the four corners of the earth.

Another mystery, akin to this, began to unfold in Solitude's loving heart. The more she learned from Wisdom, the more Solitude's heart was filled with people. After some years, there were thousands. Some of them she had met in person. But most—by far the majority—she had known in the light of the Fire that burned within her. It had become so strong a flame that she kept begging Wisdom to let her go to the land of her dreams, lest she die of waiting. She sang again to the Wind: "How long?" Finally, one day, Wisdom granted her friend's request. She blessed her with a strong and beautiful blessing—the same as the blessing given to incense: "May you be blessed by the One in whose honor you shall be consumed."

The blessing burned deep in Solitude's heart. She was already feeling a bit old when she and her friends brought the Fire across the sea in a rickety boat. Five years later, she felt ancient. She wrote to Wisdom, "My hair is grey, I have no teeth, and my hands are roughened by weather and work." More to the point, Solitude seemed to grow poorer and poorer with age. Most of her beautiful dreams were broken beyond repair. It was not easy, that land beyond the sea.

Years passed again and she grew old and tired and patient. Her heart yearned for a word from Wisdom, her friend, but the voice on the Wind was silent. She felt abandoned and useless. But, on spring days, one dream yet stirred in her heart, a dream like a glowing ember, almost banked in ashes. The people who lured her across the sea called her still. She would go to them once before she died.

The journey was long, and it almost finished her. She could not speak to those she loved. So she spent her days before the Great Fire, and warmed them all with the Flame that consumed her. And they saw the Fire in her eyes when she looked at them. And they felt the Fire in her trembling old hands when she blessed their children. And they watched the Fire glow in her as she came and went. And they knew that she was not really Solitary. For they themselves, and many to come, were all her children.

So, they gave Solitude a new name. They called her "The Woman Who Prays Always." They knew that she was blessed by the Fire that consumed her. And they knew that they were blessed by that very same Fire.

One day, at the end of her journey, Solitude breathed her last. The Wind of the plains took up her breath. It sang for joy in the oak trees of many lands, lighting the fire again and again. Even to this very day.

The Signal Grace

Elizabeth Walsh, RSCJ
To a meeting of Associates
November 18, 2008

On February 9, 1818, Philippine and her four companions said good-bye to Madeleine Sophie, the community in Paris, and to her beloved family, many of whom lived in the city. This marked the beginning of a six-month journey that would take them from France to Saint Louis. For all except Eugénie Audé, this journey would last for the rest of their lives, as she was the only one who ever returned to France.

Before leaving her homeland, Philippine was occupied with the many details that preparation for a long journey requires. Among these occupations and, perhaps blessed, distractions, she took some time to write a letter to her community at Sainte-Marie d'En-Haut. In this letter she spoke of the past and implored forgiveness for her many faults, at least as she saw them. Then she wrote of the sacredness of this moment in her life and of the future. This is what she wrote:

> Ordinarily (God) gives one outstanding grace to a soul, and this grace becomes the source of many others. In my case that signal grace was my return to Sainte-Marie and membership in the blessed Society of the Sacred Heart. This was far beyond anything I hoped for. And still—in spite of the fact that I have profited so poorly by all the instructions and the examples of solid and sublime virtue I have received—still God in his goodness is opening to me a new career that calls forth all my gratitude and overwhelms me with confusion when I think of it. (Callan, 147).

We might have expected her to name earlier graces received through her attraction to the life of a missionary, or some gift of God received in her several stays in Sainte Marie. But when she wrote of the "signal grace" of her life, she did not recall her initial attraction to mission life, nor the many graces she had received at Sainte-Marie—as a student and later as a novice. Instead, she referred to her meeting with Madeleine Sophie Barat in 1804 and her decision to join the fledgling congregation dedicated to the Sacred Heart of Jesus. Philippine sensed that life in this new congregation would enable her to live a life that was both contemplative and active. She embraced the new form of religious life for which Sophie was struggling at that moment and would for some years to come. Her followers would not be confined to one monastery for life, a convent that was more or less autonomous and separate from other institutions of the same order. Sophie's vision was for a Society composed of multiple foundations that would be united under one superior general and devoted, through the work of education, to discovering and making known the invincible love of God made incarnate in God's son Jesus. Philippine must have realized that in some way this new life would give her more opportunities to make her own love of God incarnate.

What were some manifestations of her own incarnate love? First of all, Madeleine Sophie, who, despite the fact that she was ten years younger, became for Philippine a mother, a sister, and a friend. Their friendship was the mainstay of her life. The correspondence they carried on when they were separated by the Atlantic Ocean gave vitality and inspiration to each. Despite the difficulties of communication, the months, sometimes even a year of waiting for an answer, Philippine cherished the letters of the mother general. She looked forward to sharing the joys and difficulties of life in the New World with Sophie and seized every opportunity to send a letter back to France. The day before Philippine died, Anna du Rousier arrived in Saint Charles to give the dying saint a last blessing from her friend and guide. This seems to have been God's own affirmation of their love and friendship.

Throughout her life she kept in touch with members of her family. When she learned of the death of Aloysia Jouve at the age of twenty-five, her sister's daughter who was also a Religious of the Sacred Heart, she wrote to Father Louis Barat, "... Our Mother... gave me news of the agony my dear Aloysia is enduring. But when one is out here on the other side of the ocean, one can only hope to see one's loved ones again in heaven. It is there I picture them all ..." (Callan 235). When she learned of the death of her dear friend and cousin Josephine de Savoye-Rollin, she wrote to her niece Amélie Jouve, "God, who saw that her soul was ready for heaven, took from her the consciousness of her approaching end, for she had always feared death" (479). This gives some insight into the conversation these friends had had in earlier years.

She was a loving superior and mother to those in her community. Octavie Berthold wrote to Madeleine Sophie:

Charity binds us closer and closer to our Mother Superior. I obey her, but my love for her is so great, it may deprive me of the merit of obedience, for it sometimes makes my motive too natural (235).

Philippine herself once wrote to Sophie about an illness of her own from which she was recovering, but went on to lament a fall suffered by Octavie:

Scarcely had I begun to regain some strength when Mother Octavie, shod in her beautiful new black velvet shoes that had just come from France and had very slick soles, slipped and fell and broke a bone in her leg; now she will be in bed thirty or forty days (231).

It is difficult to imagine "beautiful black velvet shoes" in Florissant, but Philippine makes no comment about the gift; she is concerned only for her daughter in Christ.

She loved the children in the schools she founded, and as we all know, she had a special predilection for the "Indians" or Native Americans. Her goodness and generosity to the Jesuits in Florissant are proverbial, and despite the rector's severity, nothing prevented her from continuing to love and nurture the Jesuit novices and to contribute to the welfare of the superior, Father Charles Felix Van Quickenborne. These relationships lasted until the end of her life. Two of the novices, Peter De Smet and Peter John Verhaegen, were instrumental in her going to Sugar Creek, and Father Verhaegen said her funeral Mass.

Her heart grew and expanded in the New World, but as these few examples illustrate, it was a suffering heart. Nor did she hesitate to take on the most practical, mundane, and menial tasks at Saint Charles and Florissant. It was she who often took care of the cows, or the chickens, or the hogs.

"How do I love Thee, let me count the ways." She might have written her own sonnet to her beloved Lord and reached an even greater depth than did Elizabeth Barrett Browning in her beautiful tribute to her husband.

The signal grace—the source of many others.

Can we name the "signal grace" of our own lives, that grace that becomes the source of many others? Let us look for a moment at the principle of life in the natural world. Life leads to fruition and to growth. We see this in the tiny buds springing from the branches of a tree, a bush, a plant of any kind. This kind of growth mirrors the pattern in human life. How many lives evolve from the union of one man and one woman? Think of your great-great grandparents. The surging life of nature is analogous to the life of the Spirit. Even in God there are three persons, and we attempt to explain this by saying the Father begets the Son; the love of Father and Son breathes forth the Holy Spirit. God is relational. So it should be expected that God's life in us will be ongoing, outgoing, and fruitful.

The seminal grace of our lives may be a realization that one has met the friend and spouse of one's life; it might be the birth of a child; it could be a change of direction or a friendship. For some of us, it has been a vocation to religious life or to the priesthood; for some of you here this evening, it may be the call to become an Associate of the Society of the Sacred Heart. It might also be a call within a call as that vocation begins to unfold. All of these gifts grow and develop through the journeys of our lives. All of these gifts involve the crossing of boundaries, probably not one as extreme as Philippine's crossing to America, to the frontier, to a new culture, a new world. But we do cross boundaries: from the limits of self to embrace the experience of the Other; from the limits of our culture to recognize the gifts of another culture; from insecurity and doubt to faith; from self-absorption to love.

In one way or another, through one experience or another, God will draw us to love. We are called to an ever-deepening love. What might Philippine have to say to us this evening? Perhaps she would borrow the prayer of Saint Paul:

> I bow my knees before the Father, from whom every family in heaven and on earth takes its name. I pray that, according to the riches of his glory, he may grant that you may be strengthened in your inner being with power through his Spirit, and that Christ may dwell in your hearts through faith, as you are being rooted and grounded in love. I pray that you may have the power to comprehend, with all the saints, what is the breadth and length and height and depth, and to know the love of Christ that surpasses knowledge, so that you may be filled with all the fullness of God (Eph 3:14-19 *New Revised Standard*).

A Life of Prayer
and Contemplation

God in the Nitty-Gritty

Therese Downey, RSCJ
November 1997

THE TWO READINGS IN today's Mass aptly describe the life of Saint Philippine Duchesne, I think. The first reading from Isaiah describes the joy a messenger of God experiences as he or she goes forth bearing the good news of God's love for all of us.

This is the joy Philippine experienced as she left France in 1818 as a missionary after many years of waiting and praying. Her dream from childhood was to bring the knowledge and love of God to the American Indians. As she boarded the ship to bring her to America with four RSCJ companions, her hopes were high, her spirit filled with joy.

The Gospel reading of today is more somber. In the invitation to follow him, Christ challenged Philippine and challenges us. Are you willing to experience with me the sufferings I went through to bring God to others? he says.

Are you willing to die to yourself and your hopes and plans like the tiny wheat seed that is buried in the darkness so new life can come forth?

This was the challenge Philippine and her companions faced as they reached American soil bringing the good news that Isaiah spoke of.

The first challenge was to their faith and obedience. The bishop who had invited them to the United States to serve the Native Americans had changed his mind. They were to start schools for the settlers instead. With faith and courage they began a small school in a log cabin in Saint Charles, Missouri. Here they shared in the hardships that other pioneer women were experiencing.

There were many trials and tribulations, but gradually the schools increased, including the schools in Grand Coteau. Vocations came, and ultimately, missionaries were sent to Cuba, Mexico, Canada, South America, and New Zealand, but before those came a mission with the Potawatomi Indians in Sugar Creek, Kansas.

But Philippine didn't personally establish all these missions. Rather, she was the hub of the wheel, as it were, giving direction, faith, and courage to the other sisters.

Why did the church canonize Philippine? It was not because of any worldly success or accomplishments. The church holds her up to us as a role model because of her faith and prayer, which enabled her, like the grain of wheat, to continue to seek God's plan for herself and for those for whom she was responsible, even though her own hopes and plans were thwarted. Her prayer was hard, but she persevered with faith. She felt she was a failure and not capable of the responsibility she was given. She was not able to learn the English language or the Potawatomi language. Accepting, with much suffering, her own limitations, she surrendered herself completely to the transformation that God was working in her own being. She was canonized because she dealt with all the nitty-gritty stuff of everyday life with faith that God is in every part of her life. She brought all of this to prayer, whether prayer was easy or hard. Her faith helped her to trust God completely, as the responsorial psalm today tells us: "I keep the Lord before me always, for with God at my right hand nothing can shake me."

Today, as we reflect on Saint Philippine's life, let us ask her to pray for us that, like her, we may go forth in joy announcing the good news of salvation, and like her, we may find God in the darkness and nitty-gritty of our lives.

"A Tree Has Hope"

Carmen Smith, RSCJ
The Rosary, 1976

A tree has hope,
if it is cut down it will sprout again
and fresh shoots will not fail.
Though its roots grow old in the earth,
and its stump die in the dust,
at the same scent of water it may break into bud
and put forth branches like a young plant (*Job 14:7-9*).

"HEART OF OAK" WE say of Philippine, and we forget the tender sapling from which it sprang—the vivacity and charm of her French youth laid gladly at the feet of Christ for whose love she climbed the mountain to Sainte-Marie. She had run and laughed on these slopes. Her life would be rooted and uprooted here—cut by her father's anger, torn away by the Revolution, only to grow green in secret and sprout again when the storm had passed.

"At the scent of water it may break into bud." Long slow tears of waiting—waiting so difficult for her high-spirited desire—gave way to tears of joy. The Lord for whom she had waited gifted her with joy flowing from the living waters of his heart. Twice she flung herself at the feet of Madeleine Sophie to give herself, first to the Society and then to us.

"A tree has hope." Nothing dimmed her desire. She came and knelt to kiss our delta dust and to put forth new branches rooted in our earth.

"Though its roots grow old." In frontier soil and frontier toil the growth was slow and silent. Poverty, loneliness, and failure challenged courage and cut at the tree. Still, "at the scent of water" flowing from the pierced Heart of Christ in prayer and Eucharist, the tree put forth branches like a young plant.

Philippine, remind us of the green and growing moments. Take us with you beyond the pain and winter cold to see you always young in heart. Let us stand with you on the frontiers of our fears, sure, as you were, that *now* is the acceptable time. Touch us with your gallant spirit, which kept its youth to the very end when you ran lightly as a girl to the God of your joy. Your smile fills the words you left us as your heritage: "I give you my heart, my soul and my life—oh, yes, my life—generously."

Make us daughters of such a mother, Heart of Jesus. Keep us supple in spirit, growing in hope, rooted in your heart. At the scent of water, may the oak break into bud and put forth new branches as when it was first planted in America in the strong young heart of Philippine.

Devotion to Daily Duty

Jan Dunn, RSCJ
Duchesne Academy, Houston

ROSE PHILIPPINE DUCHESNE WAS the Religious of the Sacred Heart who brought the Society of the Sacred Heart to the United States in 1818. The church canonized her as a saint on July 3, 1988. Our school here in Houston is named after her: Duchesne, which means "Heart of Oak" or steady heart.

Gavan Duffy, one of her biographers, was to ask the question: "What have we learned from her?" One of his answers was: "The power of grace released by deep divine desires and simple duty, daily done."

In that answer, I think, Duffy has named two elements of being Sacred Heart, namely, being a spiritual person and doing one's daily duty; we must be in relationship with God, live out of our faith, work with God, walk with God, have influence with God, and we must do our daily duties with zeal and love.

There are many stories about Philippine, some almost myths; but most of her life was like ours, performing routine daily tasks. One of my favorite stories of Philippine illustrates her performing her daily tasks. Often at night when all the students were in bed, Philippine would collect their stockings and darn them. Because she had not learned much English and therefore could not do much teaching, but being quite a good needlewoman, she did what she could.

As Sacred Heart educators, parents, and alumnae, we too are called to do what we can, to use the gifts we have been given. The lesson here is to rely constantly on God's grace as we educate the children, each and every one who comes to us: to listen to them, to communicate with them, to form relationships with them, to find modern ways to "darn their stockings."

Although Philippine did simple duties day in and day out, she was a risk taker and saw many changes in her lifetime. Being forced from her Visitation convent, she entered the Society at age thirty-five. She left France at age forty-eight to come to the new world, and what a change that was! Living in the little pioneer towns of Saint Charles and Florissant in the 1800s, towns that hardly reached the level of civilization of France at that same time.

She opened schools and sadly her beloved Florissant closed. She finally reached her dream of going to teach the Indians at age seventy-two, only to have to leave a year afterwards. Yes, Philippine saw many changes in her life.

Let us pray to emulate Philippine's devotion to daily duty and openness to change.
May our hearts be as intrepid as hers in crossing boundaries,
as generous as hers in carrying out our daily tasks,
as faithful as hers in planting seeds whose fruit we will not see.

A Preference for Poverty

Sally M. Furay, RSCJ
November 16, 2009

FOR THOSE WHO ARE aware of the life and work of Rose Philippine Duchesne, the two passions of her life are evident: her meeting in 1804 and lifelong relationship with Madeleine Sophie Barat, founder of the Society of the Sacred Heart; and her early calling to serve the Native Americans in the fledgling country across the Atlantic from her native France.

Rather than focusing on these well-known facts, I want to explore another aspect of Philippine's mission, evident throughout her life both in France and in the United States, and clearly integrated with her friendship with Sophie Barat and her vocation to serve Native Americans. Today's reading from Isaiah proclaimed that "...the Lord has comforted the people, and redeemed Jerusalem," while the Gospel reminded us that "Whoever serves me, the Father will honor." From this scriptural point of view, Philippine's constant preference for comforting and giving service to others could be called a forerunner of the late twentieth/twenty-first century prominence of "solidarity with the poor"—in spite of her nineteenth century self-denigrating attitudes and her strong sense of failure.

In France, when Philippine, age twenty-three, was forced by the French Revolution to leave her beloved Visitation convent, this wealthy, upper class woman from one of the most politically and financially well connected families in Grenoble, chose a life of independent service to the poor and dispossessed for the next twelve years. As one biographer points out, "She would change her place of residence repeatedly, initiate a variety of charitable works, some of which were dangerous and all short-lived; ... disconcert her family; and finally, anger and alienate her former Visitation sisters."

She devoted her inheritance and continuation of her work for the needy. Concerned relatives, who wanted her to behave like a gentlewoman from a prominent family and follow the safe, widely accepted modes of charitable help and contributions characteristic of women of her class, urged her to be sensible and avoid the risks of associating with the unfortunate and the poor and priests in hiding in revolutionary France. She assured her critics that it made her happy to serve Christ in this way, recognizing the presence of God in the oppressed; Eucharist and the poor were both Christ's body for Philippine. It was part of her character throughout her life not to tolerate half-way measures, and she was vocal about it!

After a hiatus of fourteen years, during which Philippine helped the growing Society of the Sacred Heart in France, she finally persuaded the founder to send her to America and her beloved Indians. Or so she thought! Though she was not to have the opportunity to be with Native Americans on their tribal lands for another twenty-three years, Philippine's education by fire during the French Revolution influenced her orientation towards the poor in the American Midwest.

A thread of concern for the poor runs through Philippine's approach to new works, closures, and opportunities during her thirty-four years in the United States. She thoroughly internalized the focus in the Society of the Sacred Heart's earliest Constitutions, which read: "If they are allowed to have any special preference with regard to the children educated or instructed in their houses, it is evident that this predilection would be just and praiseworthy if it is directed towards the poor children . . . ; they must therefore consider it a privilege to be employed in classes for the poor, whose state of life had such charms for the Heart of Jesus that He chose to be born, to live, and to die in extreme poverty." (Const. 1815, 96. VIII).

This woman, brought up in luxury in the south of France, embraced poverty in her personal habits. She resisted going to more affluent Louisiana, insisting that she would not fit in with that style of life, as she wrote later to Mother Barat: "My heart leans always to the side of the less fortunate, and that is Missouri," where the houses were struggling and poor. After an early foundation at Saint Charles, Missouri, where the boarding school initially failed, Philippine was strongly attached to the free school for the poor there, and tried unsuccessfully to find funds to keep it open. Her joy knew no end when, in 1828, the Society returned to Saint Charles, its cradle in 1818. Later, in Saint Louis, where numerous students flocked to the free school for the poor, even when the boarding school was struggling, Philippine opened a special Sunday school for mulatto girls who were otherwise excluded from education in the slave state of Missouri.

In 1825, just seven years after her arrival in America, Philippine established a separate boarding school at Florissant for Indian girls, begging money from her family and from Mother Barat to maintain it. But those were the years when the United States government was buying or seizing tribal lands and pushing Indians farther west, too far from families for the Indian girls—so the overall effort failed. Back in France, the superior general, Mother Barat, recognized and admired the role of Philippine in fostering in the United States the significance for the Society itself of what we now call solidarity with the poor, a constituent element of the mission of the Society of the Sacred Heart.

As is well known, Philippine, with the assistance of friendly Jesuits, was finally able to spend close to a year of her life on tribal lands with the Potawatomi in today's Kansas. At Philippine's canonization in 1988, members of the Potawatomi tribe brought up the gifts at the Offertory to honor "The Woman Who Prays Always," still remembered by the tribe. Because of declining health, Philippine had to return to Saint Charles in 1842.

In her final years at Saint Charles, Philippine retained her emphasis on helping the poor. A thank-you letter to her family in France indicated her joy in their gifts, which enabled her to make vestments for very poor churches. Even a little over a year before her death, she was still focused on her beloved poor, writing to Mother Barat from Saint Charles that "In spite of all the difficulties, we shall always have day pupils who pay a little, the poor children who have no other chance for education, and some boarding pupils from the vicinity. ..."

Several years earlier, her much-loved RSCJ niece Amélie Jouve had visited her, and described Philippine's personal legacy of poverty in a letter to Saint Madeleine Sophie: "You would be deeply touched, Reverend Mother, by the poverty of Saint Charles. It could hardly be greater. Mother Duchesne's room is a veritable sanctuary of this virtue. Certainly in the whole Society there is no one more poorly housed or clad or shod. ... And it is quite useless to argue with her in this matter—it is her attraction."

Philippine's Dream

Shirley Miller, RSCJ
Academy of the Sacred Heart, the Rosary
November, 1993

WE ALWAYS CLAIM PHILIPPINE here in the South because, after three months at sea, when she and her four RSCJ companions came from France, she landed right here in New Orleans on the Mississippi River. Her first act when she disembarked from the boat, was to kneel down in the muddy, murky, swampy soil and kiss it, in gratitude for their safe arrival and in hope for all that lay ahead of them. Our annual lower school play on Philippine's feast gives us some insight into her journey across the sea—the quick goodbyes to her family and friends, her RSCJ sisters, all people she loved deeply and would never see again; the long, arduous journey, sea sickness and storms and homesickness. She left everyone, everything she loved because she had a dream and was willing to sacrifice all of it because of her dream, that dream that she knew was God's dream as well, to bring the love of the Heart of Christ to the Native Americans.

We all have dreams. What are we willing to sacrifice for them? What seas are we willing to cross to follow our dreams? What muddy, murky, swampy soil are we willing to kiss? Dreams fulfilled come with a cost. There was the patient waiting, waiting, waiting for the moment when she would receive permission from her dear friend, Madeleine Sophie Barat, to cross the sea to America, the patient endurance once she arrived, waiting thirty some years before she was able to live among her beloved Potawatomi. Today we find that kind of waiting almost unacceptable—if we can't get on line right away, if we have to wait in line at carpool or when we are walking behind an elderly person or have to wait in the cafeteria line for French fries at lunch.

The cost of Philippine's dream was sacrifice and prayer. The Potawatomi called her the "woman who prays always."

There is a story by Rabbi Israel Friedman about a small Jewish village far off the main path: Once upon a time there was a small Jewish village that had all the necessary facilities: a law court, a hospital, a cemetery, as well as the usual assortment of craftsmen—shoemakers, tailors, bakers and carpenters. The village, however, lacked one trade, a watchmaker. Over many years, the clocks in the town became annoyingly inaccurate, and many of their owners stopped winding them and just ignored them. However, there were a few people in the village who believed that as long as their clocks were running, they shouldn't be discarded. Day after day, they wound their clocks, even though they no longer kept the correct time. Their neighbors made fun of them. "How silly to keep winding your clock when it doesn't keep accurate time." But one day the good news traveled like lightning: a master clock maker had just moved into the village. Everyone rushed to his house with the clocks. To their dismay, they discovered that the only ones he could repair were those that had been kept running, for the abandoned clocks had grown too rusty to fix.

And thus, our lives of prayer ... do we take time to pray daily, to wind our clocks, whether or not we feel any response from God? If God's response seems annoyingly slow or inaccurate, do we hang on, like Philippine, like the wise villagers, trusting that in God's time, our prayers will be answered. Do we take advantage of our beautiful surroundings, our chapel and gardens and city, to go apart for a few moments of gratitude? Do we take Jesus' words seriously, "Ask anything in my name, and I shall give it to you?" We cannot count on hearing God's response at age sixty-five if we grow rusty when we are eighteen.

In preparation for Philippine's feast, this is what I ask her for each of us in this chapel—that wherever we are, however we feel, whatever the color of our soul this day, we will be women and men who pray always, who keep our clocks wound, who trust that the watchmaker will come to our village if we believe.

Lord God, may we imitate the spirit of Philippine who surmounted every obstacle to be about the work to which you called her, with courage and confidence.

May we imitate the spirit of Philippine who with unfailing confidence in God endured daily privations and misunderstandings in order to fulfill her dream for the children of America.

May we imitate the spirit of Philippine who reached beyond cultural, language, religious differences to spread the love of the Heart of Christ.

May we imitate the spirit of Philippine, who never gave up in spite of discouragement and failure, who kept on loving, believing, hoping, praying because she never lost sight of her dream, nor of you, her beloved God.

May we imitate the spirit of Philippine, who saw in the difficult child or the demanding adult the work of grace and the call to love.

May we imitate the spirit of Philippine, who did all in her power to keep those with whom she worked united in their convictions and united in their love for the sake of the children entrusted to her care.

Lord, teach us to pray—always.

Transformed by the Cross

Denise Pyles
November 18, 1994
Texts: 2 Cor 5:14-17, Psalm 63, John 12:20-26

LAST YEAR I HAD the privilege of being in Saint Charles—the holy ground that received the seeds of Philippine and her dreams, as well as the seeds of the Society in this land. Philippine's spirit and presence were very real to me while I was there. Now this good fortune of being at Saint Charles came however at a great price—teaching eighth graders. It was the longest and most difficult nine months of my life. Every school day in the early morning I would go to the Shrine and pray—pray for the grace to make it through the day—one nanosecond at a time. The Shrine was a place of solitude and strength for me. Sometimes I wondered though if Philippine was the patroness of Murphy's Law. Teaching did not get any easier as the year went on. The year became more relentlessly frustrating and difficult. I wondered again if Philippine was the patron saint of doom and gloom. So much for good news. But each day I would go to the Shrine and pray, asking Philippine to pray for me—a monumental task that would keep her busy for a while. While I prayed, I sensed that Philippine kept pointing to the cross in the Shrine. It was as if she said, "This, this was the way." She is often quoted as saying, "Let us bear our cross and leave it to God to determine the length and the weight." Well, the year trudged on for me. In December, I began counting the days. Still, I visited the Shrine every morning and somehow was gifted with the grace and strength to make it through another day. In the spring, the same passage from tonight's Gospel grabbed my heart.

"Unless a grain of wheat falls to the earth and dies, it remains just a single grain; but if it dies, it bears much fruit."

The passage stirred within me a hope that something deeper was going on than just teaching eighth graders for the year. Possibly a transformation was beginning. And Philippine—she, too, inspired me with hope and courage to live my dreams.

In tonight's readings we hear of the paradox of the Cross. Paul reminds the Corinthians to model the love of Christ, a new life in Christ that is other-directed. Jesus speaks to his disciples that his hour has come, the culmination of his mission is near. Jesus' death makes salvation possible for others. The seed does not remain alone. We are reminded that suffering and loss are part of the journey of discipleship. "Those who love their life lose it. ..." We are also reminded that we are not alone. Jesus identifies with us. "Whoever serves me must follow me, and where I am, there will my servant be also."

On this feast of Philippine, we remember that she was all too familiar with the "good cross" as she called it. She cultivated a spirituality of suffering all throughout her religious life. She was a saint who suffered. Catherine Mooney says that "she felt both the joy of God's presence and the pain of God's absence." She was a saint who was stubbornly faithful. The paradox of Philippine's life, like the paradox of the Cross, was that she was a woman filled with hope in the Resurrection. Her faithful persistence enabled her to become a new creation. She lived no longer for herself, but for others. She enfleshed the Paschal Mystery.

The readings tonight and the life of Philippine are clear: to live as a Resurrection people, we must be willing to embrace the Cross, the fullness of the Paschal Mystery. Discipleship does not come with a lifetime warranty of cheap grace.

Tonight we gather at table as a community of disciples. We gather to feast upon the love of Christ. For it is the love of Christ that urges us on. The love of Christ moves us outward so that we may live no longer for ourselves but for others. Dare we cultivate a stubborn fidelity to live in this love?

The Eucharist reminds us again of the paradox of the Paschal Mystery. Dare we lay down the grains of our being to live in the hope of a new creation, a new life in Christ? Philippine reminds us: "We cultivate a small field for Christ but we love it, knowing that God does not require great achievements, but a heart that holds back nothing. ..."

"Very truly I tell you, unless a grain of wheat falls into the earth and dies, it remains just a single grain; but if it does, it bears much fruit."

A Woman of Vision

Elaine Abels, RSCJ
Duchesne Chapel, Omaha, 1988

LET US TAKE A few moments to reflect on Philippine's canonization, on the vision Philippine had to bring the Gospel message to the American Indians, and on Paul's prayer in Ephesians. Perhaps Philippine's prayer for each of us today is Paul's prayer:

Out of His infinite glory, may He give you the power through His spirit for your hidden self to grow strong, so that Christ may live in your hearts through faith, and then, planted in love and built on love, you will with all the saints have strength to grasp the breadth and the length, the height and the depth; until knowing the love of Christ, which is beyond all knowledge, you are filled with the utter fullness of God. (Eph. 3:16-19; *Jerusalem Bible*)

It is very timely that America should be given a new saint and that it should be Philippine. I say this for four different reasons.

Philippine was a woman of vision. America has prided herself on her vision of freedom and equality for all. I think that we are at a point in our history where we need a saint like Philippine to whom to pray, to help us expand our horizon to the rapidly changing needs of our global community today. Like Philippine, who gave up her own homeland of France and was transformed by God's action in her, perhaps we too as individuals and as a nation are called to give up certain views of our homeland. Perhaps they are images of America as a "successful nation," of America as number one, or other views that God is waiting to reveal to us in prayer. You and I are among the ten percent of the world that controls seventy-five percent of our recognized resources. We cannot grasp the breadth and the length, the height and the depth of this problem unless we have faith in Christ to expand our hearts, to transform us with His love. Then filled with the fullness of God, we will be able to open ourselves to others' points of view, to share our fullness with all people, to be receptive to new visions as Philippine was.

Secondly, Philippine lived a life of faith; she was a contemplative in action. A grandmother told me a priest once asked her how she ever managed to raise her ten children. She told him, "I never knew what to do next, but each time, over and over during the day, I would simply say to myself, 'Jesus, Mary, Joseph, come to my assistance,' and I would have the grace." This is one form of contemplation in action and we need to develop it. Our American culture shows many signs of illness. We as individuals are bombarded and encouraged to enhance our image of ourselves, to build up our egos through consumerism, through drugs, through self-indulgence. We think that this will make us happy, great and strong, not realizing that it is not our egos but our hidden inner self that needs to grow strong. God's spirit guides and strengthens the inner self through prayer and faith. The Gospel message has been carried externally across the face of America. Now let us carry it to the internal frontier of the American psyche, to strengthen the inner self so that Christ may live in our American heart. Then planted in love and built on love, we will with all the saints of other nations have strength to build and co-create a world community of peace, one in which we respect and cherish the uniqueness of every individual, and in which the resources of our world are shared among all.

Thirdly, Philippine was a woman who suffered numerous hardships at the hands of a male dominated society and Church. She was loyal to her Church but also pushed the limits of what a woman of her time could do. She learned through prayer how to give and sacrifice herself appropriately, not to allow oppression to embitter her, and to assert herself. She is a model for us.

Finally, Philippine is a patron for the elderly. She is a person who remained productive in her later years, even though she felt a failure. She arrived at the Indian mission at age seventy-two and then only for a year. Perhaps at this time and in the ten years that followed, more than any other, Christ lived in her heart through faith. America has an ever growing population of elderly. May the elderly American find strength in her example.

Ah, yes! Dear Philippine, we are proud of you today. We pray and ask you to pray with us the conclusion of Paul's prayer:

Glory be to him whose power, working in us, can do infinitely more than we can ask or imagine; glory be to him from generation to generation in the Church and in Christ Jesus for ever and ever. Amen. (Eph. 3:20-21, *Jerusalem Bible*)

New World Grit[4]

Nance O'Neil, RSCJ
November 1987

PHILIPPINE IS BEING CANONIZED at this very time in the history of the Society, and at this moment in the Society's history in the United States.

What is there about Philippine that is especially apt for us today? I hear a practical, a persevering, a prayerful woman; a pioneer prompting us. Philippine was "down to earth." She was not strong on theory; she believed in getting things done. Her life was marked by austerity, with purposefulness no matter what the cost. I call it grit.

Remember JFK saying in the early sixties: "By the end of the decade we shall put a man on the moon," and on that same day, "By the close of the decade we can eliminate hunger"? We could have done both. We could have made a new world order. Our purpose in all our works is to prepare people to create this New World Order, to people it with women and men of faith, hope, and love.

We have in Philippine a "New World" woman. Who better to pray to when we talk of "New World Order," "New Cosmology"? She "broke the boundaries," so can we. She will show us how to do away with the boundaries that bind our ability as people to put an end to homelessness and hunger, to imbalance and ignorance.

The boundaries that need to be broken are down to earth. I believe we need simple, practical, down to earth words and actions, "Philippine-ish," if you like. Philippine in her holiness can show us how to renew the earth.

"For wherever a saint has dwelt, there is holy ground and the sanctity shall not depart from it. From such ground springs that which forever renews the earth" (T.S. Eliot, *Murder in the Cathedral*).

The sanctity sprang from Philippine's prayer. Surely the Potawatomi phrase, "the woman who always prays," provides us with the ideal towards which we all strive. But this was said of her near the end of her life when the struggle between work and prayer was settled

---

4 Excerpts from the homily given to re-open the Provincial Chapter, printed in *RSCJ Newsletter*, January 1988.

by poor health and physical weakness, when holiness was hers. I like, too, to think of her prolonged prayer when she was younger, when, despite fatigue, she so prized her time with God. Remember the story of Holy Thursday night when she didn't think she'd stay awake for even one hour?

It was not the time given to prayer that made her holy, but her openness to the Person she met in prayer. Her encounters with God enabled God's power to work freely and fully in her, transforming her gradually until she came to recognize God's power at all times. She opened herself to that transforming power.

"Always we are filled with hope in our encounters, sure of God's power at work in us all" (Constitutions).

Representations

Marcia O'Dea, RSCJ
November 18, 2013

A POEM RICHARD WILBUR, poet laureate, wrote, entitled "Giacometti," a dense work, speaks of how the sculptures we make, the rock statues and commemorative stones, show we can "baffle rock, and in our will, / Can clothe and keep it." In the middle of the poem the speaker ventures into Giacometti's studio where the artist hews *The Walking Man* out of plaster—and eventually bronze; the surface of the sculpture recreates the mystery of the human figure when seen from afar, but there is no "fullness" in this figure. The "fullness is escaped / Like a burst balloon's."

Another sculpture one can see in Saint Charles is the statue of Rose Philippine Duchesne, a robust form bolstered by the grip of a child in her skirts. Contrary to Giacometti's figure, there is no diminishment represented in her figure. This statue makes a tacit claim that we need not be Giacometti's "starless walker, one who cannot guess / His will."

Central to Wilbur's poem is the power of human beings to walk. Myth and history have given a symbolic meaning to "walking," which connotes a person's whole conduct of self, his/her response to whatever or whoever leads or inspires. In Scripture walking connotes living according to God's will, to "walk in his path" (Micah 4:2). Byron's simple lines: "She walks in beauty like the night / Of cloudless climes and starry skies" indicates the woman's manner of presence and procedure. In Wilbur's poem, "walking" refers to one's intentionality, to the stance and swing phases of cogitation, to one's "tending forward." As Wilbur suggests, we come to know the persons we are in looking at sculptures, and we wonder "Where shall our feet / Come to a common stand?"

Wilbur concludes his verse saying, "And volumes hover round like future shades / This least of Man [*The Walking Man*], in whom we join and take / A pilgrim's step behind." In light of the bronze statues of *The Walking Man* and of Philippine Duchesne, we ask with earnestness and optimism where our "pilgrim step" will lead? We have in the less artful statue of Philippine, not a sign of *The Walking Man's* spiritual scarcity, but of her inner riches, not a posture "pruned of every gesture," but a presence revealing tender stamina and grace, not a face "anonymous and lonely," but a distinct visage at once warm and serious; and not a form "made of infinite farewells," but one made of continuous welcomings. As Philippine asks us to take a "pilgrim step" behind her, we venture to move forward in her footsteps.

Just as they shaped her, four dispositions guide our walking. Firstly, we seek that spirit of prayer that sculpted her into Christ, the one who "went before [her] on the narrow path;" as in faith the love of Christ found and defined Philippine, she would bid us be locked in that Love. Also, just as the Light of the Holy Spirit tempered Philippine's too adamant desires, we seek to be open to the work of this Spirit; and, finally, we strive in educative ways to draw others to a "common stand," to a place where mission leads us beyond ourselves and into community. As Nance O'Neil, RSCJ, has said, Philippine's "life says that the person for others is most fully a person, most fully the reflection of God's hope for humanity." In taking a "step behind" Philippine we create, not "railleries of rock" or "stony [shapes]" we can "bulk in air," but images of ourselves built up in that Fullness we have all received.

All That I Am

Tara Carnes

O Divine Love, my very God
Let my soul look up with a constant hope and my will be lost in you
And when the storms of life surround me, you lead the way
You guide my steps on the road ahead each and every day

All that I am and all that I have, this sacrifice of love
Offering all, keeping nothing, let it rise above
To the Heart of Jesus
Heart of Jesus
Heart of Jesus
You are my all in all

Let my love be a consuming fire
And all my dreams my very God, a breeze that fans the flame
Pour on it incense and perfume of all goodness
And to this holy sacrifice bring all that I possess

All that I am and all that I have, this sacrifice of love
Offering all, keeping nothing, let it rise above
To the Heart of Jesus
Heart of Jesus
Heart of Jesus
You are my all in all

Philippine Duchesne (1769-1852) As a Teacher of Prayer for Today

Annice Callahan, RSCJ
Talk to the Children of Mary in New Orleans
November 1, 2014

ROSE PHILIPPINE DUCHESNE, a nineteenth-century Religious of the Sacred Heart, can teach us a couple of ways to pray: one, an apostolic form of adoration and the other, a way of praying with heart wounds. Both of these approaches can help us to pray today.

Philippine can be viewed as a teacher of prayer for today. Her Holy Thursday all-night adoration of April 3, 1806, was a way of mediating Christ's heart to the wounded heart of humanity. She expanded the contemplative focus of adoration to include an apostolic focus on wounded people everywhere, especially Native Americans.

Another way she prayed was contemplating Christ's pierced heart in her own wounded heart. In other words, she allowed herself to feel her wounds, identified with Jesus in his wounds, and then offered them to God.

Rose Philippine Duchesne was a former Visitandine who, through her encounter with Madeleine Sophie Barat, became a Religious of the Sacred Heart in France in the nineteenth century. Along with four other RSCJ, she brought the Society of the Sacred Heart to the North American continent.[5]

Philippine felt drawn to serve the Native American people. She described her desire to follow Christ as a missionary: "My first enthusiasm for missionary life was roused by the tales of a good Jesuit Father who had been on the missions in Louisiana and who told us stories about the Indians. I was just eight or ten years old, but already I considered it a great privilege to be a missionary. I envied their labors without being frightened by the dangers to which they were exposed, for I was at this time reading stories of the martyrs, in which

---

5 The four RSCJ who came to North America with Rose Philippine Duchesne were Eugénie Audé, Octavie Berthold, Catherine Lamarre, and Marguerite Manteau. See Madeleine-Sophie Barat, RSCJ, and Philippine Duchesne, RSCJ, *Correspondence*, Second Part-I: North America (1818-1821), ed. Jeanne de Charry, RSCJ, trans. Barbara Hogg, RSCJ (Rome: Society of the Sacred Heart, 1989), 1-2.

I was keenly interested. From that time the words *Propagation of the Faith* and *Foreign Missions* and the names of priests destined for them and of religious in far-away lands made my heart thrill."[6] Louise Callan, RSCJ, one of Philippine's biographers, went on to write: "So Philippine cherished her desire and fostered it by prayer and acts of self-sacrifice and self-control."[7]

At eighteen years of age, in 1788, Philippine entered the cloistered Order of the Visitation at the monastery of Sainte-Marie d'En Haut in Grenoble, France, the city in which she had been born. Four years later during the French Revolution and the suppression of religious orders, Philippine was obliged to lay aside her religious habit and return to her family. In 1801, Philippine returned to the monastery of Sainte Marie d'En Haut in Grenoble in the hope of living an austere religious life with companions who were also committed to following Christ by religious vows. They were given the name of Daughters of the Propagation of the Faith.[8]

On December 13, 1804, Madeleine Sophie Barat, who had founded the Society of the Sacred Heart, made her first visit to Sainte Marie d'En Haut and was greeted by Philippine prostrate before her exclaiming "How beautiful upon the mountain are the feet of the messenger who announces peace" (Isa 52:7 NRSV). Sophie realized at once that much had to be changed at the Sainte Marie d'En Haut convent in Grenoble to make it a Sacred Heart convent: "Traditional ways of acting, customs belonging to Visitation life—and this called for tactful handling on the part of the young superior."[9] Sophie was, in fact, much younger than Philippine. They developed a soul friendship that became a gift and a strength for both of them. In 1806, Sophie was named the first superior general of the Society of the Sacred Heart. In 1806, she gave Philippine permission to spend the night of Holy Thursday in prayer.[10]

1. Holy Thursday Prayer of Mediating Christ's Heart to the Wounded Heart of Humanity

Philippine was given a Holy Thursday experience: for Philippine an all-night adoration of the Blessed Sacrament on April 3, 1806. Philippine was drawn to intercede for the wounded heart of humanity. Let us try to imagine Philippine in her context of nineteenth-century French spirituality, with her heart's overwhelming desire to be sent to the Native American people. On April 4, 1806, Philippine wrote of that night to Madeleine Sophie:

---

6 Philippine Duchesne's sketchy paragraph in Louise Callan, RSCJ, *Philippine Duchesne: Frontier Missionary of the Sacred Heart*, Abridged Edition (Westminster, Md.: Newman Press, 1965), 23.

7 Callan 23.

8 Callan 69.

9 Callan 81.

10 Callan 97.

All night long I was in the New World, and I traveled in good company. First of all I reverently gathered up all the Precious Blood from the Garden, the Praetorium, and Calvary. Then I took possession of our Lord in the Blessed Sacrament. Holding him close to my heart, I went forth to scatter my treasure everywhere, without fear that it would be exhausted. Saint Francis Xavier helped me to make this priceless seed bear fruit, and from his place before the throne of God he prayed that new lands might be opened to the light of truth. Saint Francis Regis himself acted as our guide, with many other saints eager for the glory of God. All went well, and no sorrow, not even holy sorrow, could find place in my heart, for it seemed to me that the merits of Jesus were about to be applied in a wholly new manner.

The twelve hours of the night passed rapidly and without fatigue, though I knelt the whole time, and in the afternoon I had felt I could not hold out for one hour. I had all my sacrifice to offer: a Mother—and what a Mother!—Sisters, relatives, my mountain! And then I found myself alone with Jesus—alone, or surrounded by dark, uncouth children—and was happier in the midst of my little court than any worldly prince. Dear Mother, when you say to me, "*Behold I send you,* I shall answer quickly, *I will go.*"[11]

Philippine's way of contemplating Christ's Heart was through the wounded heart of humanity. Even though her images of his precious blood and her theology of his merits might not speak to all of us, her missionary zeal to reveal God's personal love to the poorest of the poor throughout the world resonates with our preferential option for the poor and our listening attentively to the signs of *our* times as deeply and as urgently as Philippine perceived the signs of *her* times. She offers us a way to pray that is wholly contemplative, wholly apostolic.

Louise de Vidaud, a former student at Sainte-Marie d'En Haut who later became a Religious of the Sacred Heart, wrote a description of Philippine that recounted Philippine's spirit of prayer and devotion to praying the whole night of Holy Thursday. Louise wrote the following:

She taught us to offer all our actions to God. ... Her words had all the more influence with us because they were accompanied by such great virtue. An angel in adoration in the church would not have impressed us more, so reverent and recollected was she at prayer. Kneeling on the floor, upright and without support, hands clasped, she remained motionless for hours. One felt the presence of God in her. Besides the holy hours of prayer at night, which were the ordinary thing with her, each year she

---

11 Callan 98.

spent the entire night of Holy Thursday to Good Friday rapt in adoration before the Blessed Sacrament. Aloysia Rambaud, who often noticed her in the chapel as late as ten o'clock in the evening, and found her in the same place next morning, cut tiny bits of paper one Thursday night and dropped them on the skirt of Mother Duchesne's dress before retiring. "If she moves," the little imp remarked overtly, "the papers will tell me so." Hurrying to the chapel early Friday morning to gather evidence, she found the good Mother in the same posture, the papers undisturbed, so the whole night had been spent motionless. It is easy to understand why we considered her a saint.[12]

2. Prayer of Contemplating Christ's Pierced Heart in Her Own Wounded Heart

Philippine is renowned for her having emphasized the success of failure. Surely her own heart was wounded time and again, for example:

– the disappointment at the beginning of her move to North America of not being able to serve the Native American people at once,

– her sense of inadequacy as a superior,

– the harsh treatment she received from the Jesuit Father van Quickenborne refusing her Communion,

– the long lapse in Madeleine Sophie's transatlantic correspondence with her,

– her inability to communicate with the Potawatomi in their own language in her old age. [13]

Philippine contemplated Christ's pierced heart in her own wounded heart—and we are invited to do the same. It becomes a way of suffering in faith, of identifying with his passion and death. Philippine's response to her pierced-heart experiences was not to turn in on herself in disappointment, resentment, or self-pity, but rather to continue to let Christ speak and act through her, and to find joy in his presence.

One RSCJ was given a dream. During it she heard Jesus say to her: "Consecrate to me your pierced heart and hand over all your troubles."[14]

Perhaps a couple of questions can help us reflect prayerfully on Philippine as a teacher of prayer:

How do I feel drawn to mediate Christ's pierced heart to the wounded heart of humanity?

How do I feel drawn to contemplate his pierced heart in my own wounded heart?

---

12 Callan 114.

13 See Catherine M. Mooney, *Philippine Duchesne: A Woman with the Poor* (New York: Paulist, 1990), esp. 107-250.

14 Anonymous RSCJ, Dream of March 26, 2000.

Zeal for Mission

Philippine's Many Frontiers

Fran Tobin, RSCJ
University of San Diego
November 11, 1999

THIS EVENING, THE CHURCH invites us to reflect on the life of a Religious of the Sacred Heart, Saint Philippine Duchesne. I am sure that she would cringe at being called a saint, for she was most uncomfortable with anything coming in her direction that resembled an accolade.

Philippine might be a bit more at home if I said that the Church invites us to reflect on a pioneer woman called to face frontier after frontier and not all of them external ones. Philippine became a saint through an honest dealing with frontiers: her deepest desire was to spread the love of God in a country whose people needed to know this love. Quoting the Gospel of John, the Church rightly puts before us the guideline that led Philippine through the challenges, the darkness, the dying that frontiers demand.

Unless the grain of wheat falls into the earth and dies, it remains just a single grain, but if it dies it bears much fruit. (John 12:24, *New Revised Standard*)

What then were some of these frontiers, and how did Philippine handle them?

One was the frontier of a new world, which involved leaving one's homeland and all that one holds dear. It was Philippine's deepest hope to be a missionary, as she put it, to take the Good News to the Indians. For years, she had spoken to Madeleine Sophie, the founder of our congregation, about this. And so, Sophie sent this forty-eight-year-old woman to the United States to build the Society's mission there. Religious sisters and good friends, they both knew that they would never see each other again nor would Philippine see her beloved France again. *Unless the grain of wheat falls into the ground and dies . . .*

Have you ever thought: What does it mean to go to a land one does not know? To a place where you know no one? Where you do not hear your own language spoken? To take a bag and a community dream and just go? And not come back?

This is what Philippine and her four younger companions did. Just imagine what seventy days on a ship in the Atlantic would do to you, especially if you were not on an ocean liner, and for sure, the *Rebecca* was no ocean liner! But Philippine, when they got off the boat near New Orleans on the feast of the Sacred Heart in 1818, kissed the ground joyfully, while her probably embarrassed companions looked on. Tradition has it that she somewhat teasingly said: "No one is looking; you kiss it too." This was the embrace of the frontier without looking back.

That day was only the beginning of other frontiers farther up the Mississippi that Philippine handled in sturdy Duchesne fashion. The first foundation was to be in Saint Louis, then just a frontier trading post surrounded by farms and prairies, but with settlers who knew of the education of the RSCJ in France and wanted it for their children. It was Sophie's hope to provide that and what she had arranged with the bishop earlier. However, as bishops through the ages are wont to do, he changed his mind, and so the religious were sent to Saint Charles, a hamlet then, twenty miles west of Saint Louis, on the Missouri River, west of the Mississippi. This was the acceptance of the frontier that comes without looking back.

In Saint Charles, Philippine and her companions opened the first free school west of the Mississippi. Weeks later, they started a day school and a boarding school—all this in the same building. Not surprisingly, Philippine headed up the poor school which had over twenty students in the first month; the other schools for paying students grew more slowly and were the support of the free school. Imagine having to deal with all three in one building, but they did! In their free time, after teaching all day, the RSCJ dug a large garden for vegetables, gathered and carried manure to fertilize it, took care of their one cow and cleaned the stable, washed children's clothes, but met nightly for prayer and conversations during which they mended clothes. This was a frontier not of their making, but of life's making, and the religious embraced it under the steady leadership of Philippine. The letters of that time from Philippine to Sophie reflect a woman on fire, very self-effacing, but very faithful to the God who shaped her through the practical challenges of daily life and relationships. *Unless the grain of wheat falls into the ground and die, it remains alone . . .*

Many years later, after several communities and schools had been established, thanks to Philippine's practical financial sense, careful use of personnel, and care for the poor and boarding schools, Philippine faced another frontier, that of misunderstanding from some of her own sisters. There was a need for change; there were complaints. And so, in 1834, Philippine at age sixty-five was removed as superior in Saint Louis; however, at Sophie's request, she remained as superior in Florissant until 1840. And what did that mean to Philippine, who had always worried and struggled to be sure that the congregation in the United States was being faithful to the directives of the Society, guided by Madeleine

Sophie? This was the heart scar from the frontier. And Philippine let it all go. *Unless the grain of wheat falls into the ground and die, it remains alone, but if it dies, it bears much fruit.*

Age was still another frontier for Philippine, and at one point, she was truly bothered by it. She wrote to Sophie in 1837: "I dread the thought of becoming a doting old lady in second childhood before death catches up with me." A year later, in somewhat lighter vein, she wrote to her niece: "I am something of an antique, I have no desire to be considered an Egyptian mummy." Yes, Philippine was beginning to face the frontier of her own mortality.

Only as she faced this frontier was she given the gift of her life: a year with the Potawatomi Indians in Sugar Creek, actually less than a year because her health could no longer take the rigors of frontier life. But in that one year at age seventy-two, this woman earned the reputation of "the woman who prays always." She did not know the language of the Indians, but she did know the language of their hearts—for it was her language and she claimed it.

For Philippine, each frontier was a dying, each breaking-through a rising, which brought new life to herself and to others. "*Unless the grain of wheat falls into the ground and dies, it remains just a single grain, but if it dies, it bears much fruit.*" The imagery in the Gospel passage signals at once the cost and the blessing of any frontier that is embraced: a dying and a rising. Philippine's life, like the life of Jesus, the One she followed and we follow, reflects that cost and blessing.

We RSCJ in both North and South America are the result of Philippine's ability to face frontiers and Sophie's unfailing vision in which Philippine and all RSCJ share; the thousands of women, men, and children whom our ministries have touched and educated in some way since Philippine came to the United States in 1818 are the fruit; the alumnae/i of the Sacred Heart throughout this vast country, which Philippine came to know and love are the fruit; the Children of Mary spread throughout the fifty states are the fruit; and the Associates are the fruit.

So, what does Philippine's life say to us today? As we face the beginning of the new millennium, what does her life say to all of us? I think the message is clear. To be open to a frontier is to be open to the future. Face your frontiers and as you face them, let your hearts be full of hope born in the Heart of God.

A Letter to Philippine

Meg Huerter Brudney

DEAR PHILIPPINE,

Happy Feast Day! On this day, people around the world are celebrating you and your life. In your earthly humility, you may wonder why, because you thought you had failed. Just the contrary, your life was amazingly fruitful.

Your arrival in the New World ultimately resulted in thousands of vocations and schools throughout North America. I actually attended one of these schools 161 years after you settled in Saint Charles. It was a wonderful experience.

I have always been intrigued by your life, Philippine, and in awe of your unwavering courage. In order to know you better, I prayed with my imagination, an Ignatian form of prayer, to know you as more than a story in the historical chronicles of Sacred Heart education. It was a beautiful experience.

In my imagination, we greeted each other, and then I became a bystander. I walked by your side as you helped those impacted by the Reign of Terror during the French Revolution and realized the ache in your heart. I sensed your impatience to get to the New World and admired your obedience to wait. I entered the *Rebecca* after you had been on the ship for a month and was subjected to the cold, damp surroundings, faced with the rough sea and smelled the unpleasant odors. My journey into your world made you fully human and heightened my admiration. I felt the aches in your bones as a forty-eight-year-old woman on your long journey and watched you pray with complete conviction and total faith. I asked God, "Would I have had this endurance and fortitude?"

I knelt by you as you prayed and joined you in your daily, unending, thankless chores. I tasted the stale bread you spared for your companions and listened to your rumbling stomach. My journey into your world was not comprehensive, but it was powerful.

I was with you when you and your fellow sisters laughed and cried, which was something I never read in the history books. I observed your compassion through your strong, yet gentle, face.

I knelt again with you as you prayed, this time near the young Potawatomi children in Kansas. I wanted so badly to experience your complete devotion and gratitude—even though you could not communicate with the little children—and surrender to God's will.

At each encounter, I tried to imagine the courage it took to continue on your journey; how to accept the challenging, relentless life that God called you to live. I pined for your courageous devotion, and I wondered if I have a bit of your courage to always say, "Yes," to God's call.

You are a model to many in the world, dear Philippine. I have so enjoyed getting to know you better. I will pray for you, and I ask that you pray for me and all your loving children of the Sacred Heart.

With love,
Meg Huerter Brudney
Duchesne Academy of the Sacred Heart, Omaha, Class of '83
and currently Head of School

An Uncomfortable Model[15]

Clare McGowan, RSCJ

BLESSED PHILIPPINE DUCHESNE, SOON to be canonized by Pope John Paul II, was a pioneer woman, a woman of prayer, a woman for the poor, an educator of women, and a "senior citizen" par excellence.

What does she have to say to American RSCJ today and, by extension, to those whom they serve? She will not be everybody's "cup of tea," any more today than she was in her own time. Nevertheless, her life and her personality do have a message.

She is a model to the elderly, for she did not give up on the young, on herself or on an environment and culture in which she never felt at home. She fought her faults (she had very real character defects) until the day she died. However, and perhaps more to the point, she fought just as hard against her tendency to self-absorption. Most of the time she was much too busy training the students, the young nuns; caring for the house, the sick, and the dying to dwell overly much on whether she was being generous enough or affable enough. In spite of her frustration with the limitations and "glitches" in her own personality, she did not let self-cultivation interfere with the outward, apostolic thrust of her life.

Philippine had the gift of friendship, was not afraid to love special people in her life, e.g. Saint Madeleine Sophie, her cousin, and her niece; and she expressed that love in the warmest possible terms. However, she could and did leave those friends, drawn by her zeal as a missionary and the pole star of her life: The Heart of Jesus.

She came from the *bourgeoisie*, the "yuppie" class of France of that time, but she was completely detached from the things people cling to today. She was not a revolutionary. In fact, she fought her rebellious nature all her life. In doing so, she submitted to what would seem to us to be outrageous examples of male chauvinism at the hands of priests who directed her. However, no matter how much one abhors their treatment of her: refusing her holy Communion, attendance at Mass, etc., one wonders what stubbornness in her allowed them to think such penances would be salutary.

---

15 From *RSCJ Newsletter*, March 1988.

The women of Philippine Duchesne's time were educated fairly exclusively to be wives, mothers, religious, or maiden ladies devoted to good works, such as caring for elderly parents or helping their married sisters and brothers with their large families. Philippine did leave home, however, against her father's will and lived alone or with a companion in an apartment during the time between the closing of the Visitation convent by the French Revolution and her failed attempt to reopen it.

She probably could never have imagined the works that some of her American daughters are engaged in today: higher education, medicine, law, psychotherapy, urban renewal, protest movements, etc. She could not have imagined either that her daughters would sympathize with challenge to church hierarchy.

One wonders whether she would have been shocked or relieved to live in our day. Probably both. The fact remains that former students of the Sacred Heart have been or are today mayors of cities (San Francisco, Chicago, Princeton), editors of major magazines (*Life, Atlantic*), a newscaster for a major network (NBC), actors on prime time TV shows (both Kate and Allie). Students of the Sacred Heart have mothered presidents and senators, founded schools for the mentally handicapped and for research in bio-ethics, and gone to jail in the cause of nuclear disarmament and the plight of farm workers.

Her American daughters in the Society of the Sacred Heart are struggling to learn Spanish as she struggled to learn English and the language of her beloved Indians. Some will fail as she failed, but many will succeed as was the story in her own time.

Saint Rose Philippine Duchesne may not always be a comfortable model within the Society of the Sacred Heart and its extended community, but her life has wonderful lessons for us all. Ours is a time that can use all the models of womanly strength, endurance, and patience under trial and failure as it can get.

Her single-mindedness, often so annoying to herself and those around her, brought her to America. She, who failed in finite terms to adjust to the new world, was, in fact, one of its major movers and shakers.

If I Were to Have a Dialogue with Philippine Today

Maureen Aggeler
1988

IF I LET PHILIPPINE question me today about my dream, my vision of a just world, what would be our dialogue? First of all, she would want to know if I am becoming more formed by Christ's love, more and more myself as I live according to his way, struggle to realize a shared dream. Philippine would probably teach me, as Madeleine Sophie taught her, that my love for others is more important than the sacrifices I am willing to make to see my dream realized.

I would tell her that I dream of a church in which men and women created equal by God can live out that equality in peace, in mutual complementarity, and in love. That means changing the system of male dominance and replacing language that expresses a bias against women or renders them invisible. With others, I want to effect a change of attitude that will nurture and restructure the role of women in the church. Philippine would see that we do not want to worship "security" and do not fear costly discipleship. She would likely encourage us to identify our challenges and hopes within the Church, to continue to look for new ways of relating as equals, ways that hold the promise of mutuality, cooperation, and inner growth.

I would tell Philippine that I read her story with new eyes and found there a spirituality of a frontier woman. It was a spirituality that grew from a dream that was continually nurtured, a spirituality that enabled her to keep going day after day, as a woman of hope. By the time she got to her long-awaited mission with the American Indians, she could write Saint Madeleine Sophie that "to go to teach the Indian children is a grace—a gift of God, not just a service."

I'd tell her how I see that she made her way prayerfully and with discernment; she did not use violence to achieve what she wanted. Neither was she afraid to stand up to the bishop when he wanted to divide the group. She struggled with courage, not only because she had to be patient to realize her dream, but because she counted herself a failure and may have been tempted to think her dream was not what God wanted.

Philippine did not lose hope, even in the darkest times, such as waiting three years for Madeleine Sophie's letter. I'd tell her how much joy that deep and lasting bond between Saint Madeleine Sophie and herself gives me now, and I'd tell her how women today are counting on one another, supporting one another in the struggle to realize a shared dream.

In such a dialogue with Philippine, I would realize how important it is to accept limitations in approaching new frontiers. She would tell me that if I live from my hope and vision of a just world, all that I do contributes to its realization. However, in my lifetime, I may not see it.

Burning Zeal

Catherine Baxter, RSCJ
Call to Worship, November 2001

FOR THE PAST WEEK here at Oakwood, we've been making a novena in preparation for Philippine's feast, using the opening prayer of her Mass, in which we ask God to fill us with the same love and zeal that Philippine had for the spread of God's kingdom.

Shortly, in the prayer over the gifts, we'll ask God to fire us with the burning zeal that consumed Philippine—and then in the prayer after communion we'll ask to be faithful to God's desires for us and zealous for the spread of the kingdom.

Now it seems to me that zeal, zealous, aren't common words in our spiritual vocabulary today. When we describe someone as zealous, I think there's an undertone of "better watch out for her."

So, just what is it we're asking for this morning? I looked through our library in Catholic dictionaries and encyclopedias and couldn't find any entry at all—but Webster's unabridged did provide some food for thought.

It lists as one of the definitions of zeal "enthusiastic diligence," which sounds like an award given at Primes or Prize Day. And when one considers diligence as a "constant and earnest effort to accomplish what is undertaken—as persistent exertion of body or mind," then "enthusiastic diligence," although it may sound like an oxymoron, is certainly one of the distinguishing characteristics of Philippine Duchesne's life.

Just a few years after joining the Society in 1804, she began her campaign to be sent to the New World. No appeals to prudence, no statistics on the dearth of personnel and lack of funds, no warnings about the physical and emotional hardships of such a venture daunted her until, finally in 1818, at age forty-eight, she undertook her life's dream—to bring new people in new lands to encounter the love of Jesus. And at the age of seventy-three, we find her once again appealing to Saint Madeleine Sophie, "They say that in the Rocky Mountains people live to be one hundred years old. As my health has improved and I am only seventy-three, I think I shall have at least ten more years of work. Will you not authorize me to go farther west?"

What was the source of her zeal, her enthusiastic diligence?

I think we can find a clue to answering that question in today's readings. She wrote to a religious she was directing who was having a hard time, "Profit by the little trials that come to you, that is the time to make progress. I shall always recall these words quoted by a man of God when I was in a situation similar to yours, 'Unless a grain of wheat fall to the earth and die, it remains but a single grain, but if it dies it will bear much fruit.'"

Philippine learned to die to herself daily in her years on the frontier—years filled with loneliness, disappointments, failures, physical and psychological suffering all of which she felt deeply. "I feel that I am a worn-out instrument, a useless walking stick that is fit only to be hidden in a dark corner. God allows everything to deepen this impression in my soul." Yet she never lost sight of what it was all about, of what it was she had started out to do. "I cry with joy at times when I realize that in one way or another, more than one hundred people are learning to love Jesus through our efforts here. I do not know how to thank God for this."

What kept her going? I think we find that in the first reading. Because she had died to self, she put no barriers to God's love. The love of Christ urged her on, impelled her, pushed her—she wasn't trying to earn his love or prove her love for him. I don't think the source of her zeal was in her love for Christ or his love for her but in the mutual exchange, the mutual gift of self that each made to the other. Being totally, freely given left her no choice, nowhere else she wanted to be but with him, doing his work, finding her delight and joy simply being in love with him.

What might she say to us today? I think she would tell us to lighten up a bit. In the midst of all the discussions about the next provincial, the needs of the province, the revision of the government plan, we need to remember what it's really all about: what it is that we undertook when we said yes to glorifying the Heart of Jesus, to answering his call to discover and reveal his love. And then, like her, we will be ready to let God's zeal take fire in us.

A Spirituality of Mission in Today's World

Melanie Guste, RSCJ
AASH, Southern Regional Conference in Houston

IN MY DAYS AS a young student at the Rosary during the infamous decade of the 1960s, I remember one of my teachers, Sharon Karam, RSCJ, telling our class that Native Americans believed that a person did not really die until the memory of them had passed, or that they had been forgotten. That really stuck with me—then and now. Sharon's teaching about Native American beliefs returns to me as we reflect this morning on Philippine's enduring spirituality of mission and of her SPIRIT, who remains so alive and robust through our sharing of her colorful story and lasting legacy. Surely, Philippine's active and lively spirit joins us today as we continue to explore and learn from her life.

Philippine's unique person and enduring story afford persons on a spiritual path a treasure of insight for their journey. This morning, I would like to highlight seven aspects of Philippine's spirituality of mission that have taken shape in me through my own experience and, also, my continued reflection on her life.

First, Philippine's life was marked by her vigor for the mission of the Society of the Sacred Heart to share God's love and by her perseverance in sharing that mission. Today, in organizational science we refer to leaders as "mission-driven," and one might say that Philippine perfectly fits this description of a person who is intensely focused on advancing a mission, an individual who is possessed with clarity of vision and with a singleness of purpose.

Many of the "stories-we-love-to-tell" about Philippine's life illuminate a character that possessed a "not-to-be- contained" passion, a distinct vitality, and an extravagant heart for mission. Like Jesus moved by suffering of the woman who touched his garment and by the man sitting by the pool at Bethsaida, Philippine's prodigious heart for others could not ignore the suffering at her doorstep resulting from the watershed event of the French Revolution. This anguishing experience touched her at a young age and, quite simply, it opened her being "to the depths of God," as stated in our Constitutions (§8) and impelled her to action.

Secondly, Philippine responded to the immediate imperative of the needs of her world with concrete actions that were grounded in her local community. When all hell broke loose in the world around her, Philippine used the "law of the feet"—as we say in organizational science—to move them with willful intention to the scene. She went to care for the prisoners, to tend the sick, and to share food with those who were hungry.

Of the many etchings and drawings we have of Philippine, so many of them depict her crossing over by boat from one place to a new place—going from the familiar to the new and even foreign. In these images, she appears so peaceful and without apparent concern, but, now—as an adult woman—I see in these images a person who has learned to "hold her seat," through many trying and exacting times to know of God's enduring presence, God's nearness even in the dark, and of God's comfort—even on moonless nights afloat on foreign seas.

This practice of sitting with all our story—not just the peak experiences but the valleys, too, and "staying put" in the face of these difficulties is a great spiritual practice of our Sacred Heart tradition. It is one that we can learn from our sister and teacher Philippine, whose spirituality is marked by the courage she found over and over again to "stay put" during the dark and difficult times of her life.

The third feature that is noticeable to me about Philippine's spirituality of mission is how she surrendered to and actually befriended discomfort of all sorts. This aspect of her spirituality has two challenging parts: the first has to do with the concept of surrender in a world where surrender is frequently understood as *losing* and where the concept of discomfort is frequently understood as something to be avoided at all costs. As most of us have learned, the real truth of our human condition dictates to us that we do not get off so easily being comfortable all the time. Like it or not, willing or unwilling, ready or not: Life eventually does knock us out of our comfort zones. Philippine's antidote for discomfort was to befriend it—not to resist it or fight it—and this approach is another special aspect of her person and a gift of insight to those of us in mission for life. Philippine's spiritual practice was one of regular and constant deep surrender: surrendering her illusions, surrendering her limitations of language, surrendering her "dreams" and her plans to a higher, more mysterious power that was at work in her life.

Fourthly, Philippine prayed. It may seem simple, but Philippine found the floor. She found her knees. Philippine's discomfort with herself, her own sense of failure and the exigencies of the strange new world she was in pointed her in an unnatural direction—the direction of the floor! Finding our knees, or kneeling, is a place all people of faith inevitably find on the journey of life. Philippine found her knees, and I think that most of us inevitably "take the proverbial knee" in our adult journey—to pause the action and, in silence, turn and bring everything to God, his Son, Jesus, and Mary, his Mother.

For many of us, we find our knees when the pain and suffering of the world draw close to us—when we feel it in a personal way just as Philippine did so many times. Lately, it seems as though the cry of the world is breaking through into so many of our lives. Suddenly, it is *your* husband who has lost an executive position, or *your* family home devastated by hurricane winds or a flood. The cries of the world do seem to be drawing closer to home. Like Philippine, we can—ironically or essentially—discover our union with God through the cries of the world. In tough times, we must seek and discover God's nearness to us, and God's compassion rising out of the "ash heap of our situation," as Joan Chittister said, right in the midst of those struggles. This is confounding, but true.

I will never forget an experience I had shortly after Katrina hit our Gulf Coast. It was no more than one and a half weeks after the storm and things were chaotic. That morning, a group of us was unloading a huge eighteen-wheeler truck filled with emergency supplies that had come from Omaha, via the kindness of Sister Georgeann Parizek's extended family and friends. The driver of another eighteen-wheeler coming from New York City turned to me as we were unloading and said, *"Well, as soon as I heard what happened here, I just had to come down here and help. You see, I was a firefighter on the scene on 9/11, and you Louisianans were right up there on the streets serving us gumbo and jambalaya out of trucks. I know what that meant to us. I just had to come when I heard."*

That was such a beautiful moment for me. Here was this stranger who felt impelled by his sense of connection through the cries of the world and the human suffering of others to offer his help. To me, this reflects the action of God's spirit working in our world to transform it, a way that is reflected in this man's—and our—compassion, sensitivity to the needs of others (even though "far away"), kindness and *big-heartedness* that is detailed over and over in daily choices of Philippine Duchesne's life.

Determined service is a hallmark of most spirituality and, as Nance O'Neil, RSCJ, the first provincial of the U.S. Province, once observed about Philippine, Philippine did it with "grit and mysticism." This way of being in mission—with Christ's attitudes and Christ's dispositions—is why I believe Philippine continues to speak to us even today.

Lastly, I want to mention Philippine's faith as an expression of hope. As Philippine's life instructs us, many of us often do discover God's fidelity to us through the sometimes difficult twists and turns of life—through its disappointments, mistakes and missteps and the relatively few achievements of life in the end. But that is not the whole story of Philippine's life! For her story is fundamentally about her hope, which surely arose from her deep union with God and experience of Christ's Heart.

As I continue to listen to her life, I see more and more how Philippine's efficacy and, indeed, her sanctity was in *how* she lived—not in what she pursued or even achieved. Rather, her holiness was in her never failing or faltering revelation of God's love through all the times of her life, including all those times of personal uncertainty and darkness. This persistent faith in God as an expression of hope is what enabled her to express such confidence that "all will be well with us."

Here at this school of the Sacred Heart this afternoon, I cannot help but be reminded of the many young people who fill the classrooms of this school and other Sacred Heart schools in the USC Province and across the world, of the teachers and administrators—all working to continue to live out the mission of the Society of the Sacred Heart as given to us by Philippine Duchesne. To all of you and all of us here as alums and members of the Sacred Heart family, I thank you for being in mission with us and for your continued witness to God's love through the Heart of Jesus.

Letter from Philippine

Bonnie Kearney, RSCJ
November 2012

DEAR SISTERS AND FRIENDS,

This is my first electronic letter, a challenge, but I was never daunted by a worthwhile challenge; and I deeply believe communications, even from afar, through times and space, hold us closer and more united. There are several things I wish to explore with you. First, I am sure each of you rejoiced with the hosts here above at the public canonization of Kateri Tekakwitha, my, our, Native American sister in Christ. Really, there are so many more unnamed, but we all rejoice in the recognition that we hope will come to indigenous peoples through this public act.

A second thing I rejoice with you about is the coming together of the Canadian and United States provinces—more like my "new world," this large, expansive, land mass filled with people longing for the Love of the Lord to meet them in their everyday lives, joys, and sufferings. I spent the first half of my life in France and Europe and the second half in the "new world." For me, the ocean was not a barrier; for you the border must not be a barrier. We share this sense of mission regardless of the place where we are called to share our strong belief that Love builds a single world, a single Kingdom.

For my small group who came representing the Society, times were difficult, decisions did not neatly fit into known patterns. There were cultural differences that caused misunderstandings. There were losses, with sickness and deaths of religious and students. The vision, which had seemed so clear back home in France, at times seemed impossible. There may be moments when these will be your experiences and feelings too, but these things can teach you to truly count on one another. I used to write Sophie and complain that what was true for France did not fit the situations here and that we had to change to enter fully into our reality. You, too, will need that ability to let go and change for the good of the whole and the mission. Culture can be an obstacle or a richness. Clearly you will work to mine the richness that is offered with this new diversity. It really does challenge and gift us with its power to open our hearts.

I mentioned how difficult were the losses and deaths, among our own and/or parents, students, neighbors. I write in sympathy for those of you who shared these recent last journeys of sisters, friends, and family. "Unless a grain falls into the ground," a timeless message to recognize how life and death are meant to be about new life. There is pain in these losses; let it not pull you down, but forward, with renewed life. It is that life to be shared that called us into this time and place. You may feel, as I often felt, with our smaller numbers, that perhaps we were stretched too far. But when each of us looked about and saw the people who, in so many ways, cried out for the Love of God to enter their lives; we recalled how Sophie continued to expand against the limits: she was a believer. Can you be any less?

I know many of you have taken my experience of night prayer over the world to heart. I also know many of you lie awake at night wishing you could fall asleep. First, a challenge, why are you so awake? Is it overwork? Anxiety? Remember the work is the Lord's, and he would prefer you to trust him. Or, are you awake because, like Samuel, you are being called in the night? If so, I offer again my experience of prayer over the world. Lift a people, a country, a concern to the Heart of our loving God. Share the burden and the hope. The night may pass more easily united in love. Second, I feel humbled that this experience of mine has also brought this call to pray with our broken world in a new way into our schools. The European Network set up a worldwide "uniting with Philippine in prayer" initiative, inviting any school that wished, to choose a country experiencing difficulties, find out about the country, write a prayer for that country, share the findings and a prayer for the country electronically with all the participating schools. Perhaps you can do this too, exploring a part of our world that seems remote but is close to the Heart of God.

Lastly, I know many of you love that image that depicts me in my elder years kneeling in prayer among the Potawatomi. They say that people left leaves and stones on my habit, wondering if I would move without their knowing it. This image gained me the name "Woman Who Prays Always." Lately, I have reflected on that and I offer you my thoughts. I was praying in sorrow, in failure, for I could do nothing else—not speak, not really cook, not carry water. They did not see my weakness or failure. They saw strength in me, knowing my real place in the scheme of things. Your sister, Melanie Guste, recently called this element of my spirituality "finding my knees." I think it is apt, but I challenge you to look again at what is not working in your lives or plans, what seems without hope of success, and knowing as you do, that the work is the Lord's, find your knees. It may not turn everything around, but who knows what others will take from your humble need of the Love and compassion that you so wish to pass on to others.

I am delighted to celebrate with you. You think this is my feast, but it is really the feast of our mission. Today, be in touch with that mission. May your prayer lead you deeper into the Heart of our God who calls his own and wishes us to find as many ways as possible to share that love with others. May your actions lead you deeper into his compassion for one another and for all who are pressed to the margins. May your day begin with Thanks and end with Thanks, and between, be lived to the fullest.

Lovingly,
Philippine

Courage

What Is Philippine Duchesne Trying to Communicate to Us Today?

Helen McLaughlin, RSCJ
Letter to All Communities: "Canonization of Blessed Philippine"
1 May 1987

Philippine was above all a woman of profound communion. All her life, she built bridges between worlds: between Europe and America, between the worlds of rich and poor, between races: Europeans, Native American Indians, Blacks, and the new people being forged on the American frontier. In a time of war and class division in France, Philippine was peacemaker, nurturer and healer to those who suffered. In America, she offered to young women an education previously available only to young men. She opened free schools for the poor where none before had ever existed. She respected the dignity of Native Americans even as their lands were being stolen and their ranks decimated by less caring immigrants. In short, Philippine spent her whole life entering into new worlds: building bridges, striving to understand other people's experience—in a word, creating communion.
   Helen McLaughlin, RSCJ (Conference, 1988)

I FEEL IT IS important for each one of us to take up Philippine's life and to reflect on her message. She has surprised us now by stirring the surface of our immediate consciousness with extraordinary energy! What is she trying to communicate to us today? Who is she for us: a courageous, sensitive woman; a deeply prayerful religious; a lover of poverty and simplicity; a loyal, suffering daughter of the Church; a pioneer into the future who dared to go where few had gone before? She is saying something to us with urgency and insistence. ...

   Personally, what impresses me about Philippine is her ability to respond to difficult events and times; to accept and love a totally different, new country and way of life; to enter wholeheartedly into another culture, language, and system of values and to appreciate these.

   Saint Madeleine Sophie loved poverty and prayer, and Philippine followed her example with a boldness and totality that permeated her whole life. This openness to the Spirit and freedom of her whole being to respond to his call did not lead her to great success, but rather to the deep experience that the grain of wheat must fall into the ground and die, that the Lord might bring forth the harvest. Trusting in him, she gave her all.

Her goal in life was not personal holiness, but a spending of her energies to make the Heart of Christ known and loved. Her missionary élan was lived in fidelity to the Constitutions of 1815. This fidelity made her holiness and virtue authentic and real, visible to those who knew her. Today, the Constitutions of 1982 hold out to us a call to be strong women, eager to let Christ "gather together all things in Himself for the glory of His Father" (§2), a call to be prayerful and discerning; reaching out to those in need, being with those who are poor—looking always towards the horizon where new worlds wait for us to give concrete expression to the very Love of his Heart.

Our prayer for one another during these days before [her] feast . . . can strengthen us. Her example . . . can encourage us to believe more surely that "the power at work within us is able to accomplish abundantly far more than we can ask or imagine" (Eph 3:20, *New Revised Standard*).

Dare to Risk

Walter J. Burghardt, SJ
November 17, 1988

Isaiah 52:7-10
2 Corinthians 5:14-17
John 21:20-26

EARLY IN OUR CENTURY that prince of paradoxes, G. K. Chesterton, wrote: "A saint is one who exaggerates what the world and the Church have forgotten." That sentence makes sense not only of a hermit Anthony locking himself in an Egyptian tomb, a black Martin de Porres asking his superiors to sell him into slavery, all those saints who slept rarely, bathed never, ate reluctantly. It is thrillingly true of all those men and women who were "eccentric" in its literal sense: They deviated from the center, from the usual practice, the ordinary way of doing things, established methods. Put another way, they stood where your dear deceased friend John Courtney Murray placed himself—what he called "the radical center." In a word, while utterly faithful, they were willing to risk.

Such, I submit, was Rose Philippine Duchesne. On this solemn, and festive occasion[16] let me spell out my thesis in three stages: (1) risk and your saint, (2) risk and your Church, (3) risk and you. In other words, today we remember, we reflect, we resolve; we look back, we look within, we look ahead.

First, risk and your saint: We look back, we remember. Now a homily is not a history; it must center on the Mystery—on Christ and the Body of Christ. Besides, you know your history far better than I. Still, the story of your saint is significant if you are to understand, not only her but the Church and your place therein. I focus on the risk that was Rose.

---

16 The occasion was the liturgical commemoration, by the Religious of the Sacred Heart in the District of Columbia area, of Rose Philippine Duchesne's canonization, which had taken place in Rome on July 3, 1988.

To risk, the dictionary tells us, is to expose yourself to loss or injury, to disadvantage or destruction. Such was your saint. I remember that she began awfully early. She risked her father's wrath when she entered the Visitation novitiate and argued with her family from behind a grille. She risked the wrath of the French Revolution when she ministered to men and women destined for the guillotine. She risked the wrath of the state when she returned to the convent and put on the habit, only to find herself and her love alone amid the religious ruins. She risked the displeasure of your dear friend Father Varin, when he came to discuss with her the new Society of the Sacred Heart. To the impatient thirty-four-year-old woman he said: "You know, God always acts slowly." Her swift retort: "On the contrary, Scripture says He runs with giant bounds."[17]

But those risks were preparation—our Lord was preparing Philippine for the American apostolate dear to his heart and hers. I remember how this novice of thirty-five met her Sacred Heart superior, all of twenty-five. Amid all the wisdom Madeleine Sophie Barat passed on to Philippine, one gem is the riskiest of all: "You know that the greatest of treasures is the cross. A large portion is reserved for you. ... You must suffer, and suffer without consolation."[18]

I remember how, fourteen years later, a year short of fifty, the supreme risk of Philippine's life began: to transmit the spirit of her Society to the New World. On the Feast of the Sacred Heart, 1818, the small sailing vessel *Rebecca* came to anchor twenty miles below New Orleans, and Philippine knelt in the dark to kiss the soil her heart had craved for years.

I remember how swiftly the cross was erected—the cross that embraced her for thirty-four years. Strangely, no word of welcome from the bishop—explained even then by the postal service. The news that not cultured Saint Louis was to house her school but tiny Saint Charles, which Philippine saw as "the tomb of her hopes."[19] So little contact with the "noble savage" for whose salvation she had crossed the sea. The school itself was a risk: Philippine found English an enigma; books and paper, quills and pencils, were at a premium; bone-chilling cold and pitiful food; liberty-loving children without the obedience of *Sacré-Cœur* in France. "Perhaps [God] wants his missionary nuns to sanctify themselves by failure."[20]

I remember how Saint Charles closed, and the sisters moved to Florissant. Now a small log cabin less human than Saint Charles. But here the risk took encouraging shape: a boarding school, promising students, progress in learning, poise and courtesy—even a piano from France. And wonder of wonder, novices, vocations. Yet, always the cross:

---

17 See the booklet by Marion Bascom, *Rose Philippine Duchesne, Pioneer Missionary of the New World* (Purchase, New York: Manhattanville College, n.d.) 9.

18 Ibid., 11.

19 Ibid., 19.

20 Ibid., 22.

yellow fever caught on a ravaged vessel; cyclone and flood at Florissant; calumny ("They say everything about us except that we poison our children."[21]); even the risk of keeping the Missouri Mission Jesuits alive—cooking for them, sewing for them, going without basics for them, so that the De Smets could bring Christ to victimized Indians. The scary serial of my adolescence, "The Perils of Pauline" cannot compare with the perils of Philippine!

I remember the Saint Louis school that pioneered parochial and public school systems there. It too had its cross for Philippine: poverty and illness, the mystery of English, an old and tired heart. While she watched her most faithful companion die in agony, Philippine's hair turned white.

I remember that Philippine was seventy-two when she realized her heart's desire: an Indian school in Kansas. But as always, with love came crucifixion. This woman whom the Potawatomi revered as "the woman who prays always" could not teach them God's ways by word, for the language was too difficult, and her health was dreadfully frail. Wanting only to die among them, she was denied even this. One year, and back to Saint Charles. "It seems to me that in leaving the savages I have left my element, and that henceforth I can do nothing but languish for the heavenly country from which happily there will be no more departures."[22]

What do I not remember? A single word of self-pity. Dismay, yes, but never despair. Feelings of failure, yes, but never surrender. Sadness indeed, but through it all a profound joy in her belief that it is God "who gives life to the dead and calls into existence the things that do not exist" (Rom 4:17 *New Revised Standard*). Father Murray phrased it profoundly to your sisters back in 1941: Her "depressing sense of inadequacy" before her task and ideal "did not take the heart out of Philippine Duchesne. Rather, it put a heart into her, the Heart of Christ, patiently obedient unto death, even to the death of the Cross. In deepest union with Christ she went on."[23]

When she died at eighty-three, Philippine could not have seen what her "failures" would achieve: North and South America, from Australia to Zaire. Oh, she knew what God could and would accomplish: "You will see that when I am dead everything will prosper."[24] Not that she had a vision of the future. She simply lived what the Son of God had told her from the shadow of his cross: "I say to you, unless a grain of wheat falls into the earth and dies, it remains alone [merely a grain of wheat]; but if it dies, it bears much fruit" (John 12:24 *New Revised Standard*).

---

21 Ibid., 27.
22 Ibid., 31.
23 John Courtney Murray, SJ, "The Magnificence of the Heart That Can Dare Great Things," in the booklet *Philippine Duchesne, RSCJ: A Collection*, ed. Catherine Collins, RSCJ, Melanie A. Guste, RSCJ, and Anna Thompson (Washington, D.C.: Center for Educational Design and Communication, 1988) 49-53, at 52.
24 From Bascom, *Rose Philippine Duchesne*, 31.

Second, risk and your Church: We look within, we reflect. You see, Philippine Duchesne is not a saint primarily because she is different; she is a saint because she symbolizes in striking fashion what the whole Church is called to be: not only utterly faithful but willing to risk.

Philippine reminds us that the Incarnation itself was a risk. Never has the world seen, never will it see, the risks that were Bethlehem and Calvary: the Son of God born in a stable, God-in-flesh dying not with proof of resurrection but with faith in his Father. If ever our earth witnessed apparent failure, it was this man who preached eternal life and was crucified like a common criminal. The point is, Jesus not only *said* that to bear fruit the grain of wheat must die; he *was* the grain of wheat par excellence. From his death our life was born.

Philippine reminds us that Christ took a terrible risk when he had Calvary continued by men and women, all feeble and fallible, some craven and corrupt. The Church is a risk God took, and only by risking can the Church carry Calvary forward. Risk has been our destiny, our story, from the day the Holy Spirit rested on the apostles like tongues of fire, the day bruised and beaten apostles "left the council, rejoicing they were counted worthy to suffer dishonor for the Name" (Acts 5:41).

Philippine reminds us that the Body of Christ has spread through the world because countless men and women afire with the Spirit dared the impossible. Not only the canonized: thirteen-year-old Agnes challenging the Roman Empire with her blood; Boniface reforming the face and faith of Germany; Augustine and Aquinas reshaping the Christian intelligence of the West; Francis of Assisi and Jane Frances de Chantal, Ignatius Loyola and Madeleine Sophie, founders of religious congregations large and small. Not only the uncanonized in neon lights; Thomas Merton and Dorothy Day and Mother Teresa. With these the unsung millions, ordained or not, lay or religious, married or single, who have spent tears and sweat and blood to touch Christ to their acre of God's world.

Philippine reminds us that we too, all of us, are asked to walk in their footsteps, simply because these are the footsteps of Christ. Not to do exactly what they did; each age, each spot, has its unique problems, and each of us is called individually. But all of us are called to risk, because each of us is called to be Christ where we are.

Philippine reminds us that the Church of Christ languishes where the mass of Christians are content to do what they have to do, are satisfied with a minimum, do not realize that they are commanded—not invited, commanded—to love God with their whole heart and mind, soul and strength, commanded to love every human person as much as they love themselves. She reminds us that we are called to be saints.

Philippine reminds us that the joy that, Christ promised, no one can take from us is impossible without the cross—Christ's cross and our own. The Christian message is still life through death; only by losing your life for Christ's sake will you find life.

Philippine reminds us that we are not called to be successful but to be faithful, and to be faith-full is to risk, literally, all.

Third, risk and you. By "you" I mean the Religious of the Sacred Heart. Not exclusively, for others dream your dreams and participate in your apostolates. I simply want to be daringly direct.

I have known you for half a century—ever since that day in '38 on Convent Avenue in New York, when the new kid on the whiz block, rising young Jewish philosopher Mortimer Adler, addressed the graduating class on, I believe, "Measure, Weight, and Number." I have been privileged to touch you from Purchase through Saint Louis to San Francisco. I have watched you struggle to link fidelity to your foundress with the demands of a new age— education then and education now. I have seen you change (the word has an honorable Christian history). Not only in externals—turtlenecks and pocket money, travel and TV— but change that cuts at the vitals of your vocation. You know the neuralgic changes more intimately than I—from a new Manhattanville to a general chapter that focused your apostolate on peace and justice, on a preference for the poor, on the Third World.

You have dared to risk, to expose your Society to loss, injury, disadvantage, even destruction. Knowing some of you, I know how delighted many of you are in your re-formation. But not all your friends have been happy—not even all your own sisters. If your Society is anything like mine—and from your birth you have been remarkably close to us—there are those among you, as among us, who have felt such anguish in changes so drastic that they cry out: "This is not the Society I entered, not the Society in which I vowed obedience." And for some the pain is so poignant, the hurt so heart-wrenching, that they must bid farewell as to a loved one who has died.[25]

It is not the right of the homilist to *appraise* your risk. Time alone will reveal to your heirs and descendants whether the risk was worth the price. What moves me mightily is your *readiness* to risk. To risk all for the heart of Christ as you hear it beat today, for the Church as it summons you at this moment in its mission, and for the most impoverished among God's people.

Here I return you to your dear Philippine. Time alone has put her "failure" in perspective. If you could tear her away for a moment from her endless partying with the angels, if you were to fix her gaze on the Children of Mary in America and on the countless children of God you have served these 170 years, if you were to say "See what your risk has wrought, what your 'failure' has fashioned," Philippine would glow with delight but answer "*Moi?* I? Not really. I merely let God be God. For all my love for the 'noble savage,' I never told God 'It's the Potawatomi or it's no go.'"

Good friends of the Sacred Heart: your own Sister Cooney, in a profound meditation on Philippine[26] asked what she would be doing if she were among us today. After all sorts

25 For details see the recent work by V. V. Harrison, *Changing Habits* (New York: Doubleday, 1988).
26 Madeleine Sophie Cooney, RSCJ, "Meditations on Philippine Duchesne," in *Philippine Duchesne, RSCJ, A Collection* (n. 8 above) 63-66.

of possible activities, from the victims of civil war in Nicaragua, through the feminist revolution in the States, to the deadly disease of AIDS, Sister Cooney recalls two temptations you must resist in a time of transition: disowning the past and simply repeating it. No, she insists, you have a much more difficult task. You must assimilate the past so as to move more creatively into the future: "an enormous and exhausting and often frustrating, ever hopeful and obstinately determined effort of creative imagination."[27] Philippine would agree. "Be faithful but free. Dare to risk. Dare to be Christ—not to the Paris of 1800 or the Sugar Creek of 1841 or even the Manhattanville of 1938. Dare to be Christ to your own world, as God gives you in community to see it. Above all, let God be God. Let the Heart of Christ be your heart."

National Shrine of the Immaculate Conception
Washington, D.C.
November 17, 1988

---

27 Ibid., 66.

The Grain of Wheat

Eileen Bearss, RSCJ
November 22, 2004

WHEN READING THE GOSPEL text for this Mass, I was struck by the phrase "unless a grain of wheat falls into the earth and dies, it remains just a single grain; but if it dies, it bears much fruit." (John 12:24 *New Revised Standard*)

It struck me that this is so true in the life of Philippine. It wasn't for her "a grain of wheat." It was an acorn and it became a mighty oak, because her name, Duchesne, means "from the oak." The seed goes into darkness in the soil where it is planted and then over time begins to change, to break open, to sprout new life with the possibility of a rich harvest. Sometimes the young plant is transplanted, and so further change is needed, leading to transformation in Christ.

We are familiar with the words of the song we sing each feast day: "Strong was her heart … and you were ready Philippine to let God's zeal take fire in you."

So with both the Gospel passage and the feast-day song, it is the two-fold movement of "letting go" and letting the fire of God's love take hold of us, letting the seed become new life true to the mission of God and yield a rich harvest. Letting go is not easy, whether it is our own agenda, our possessions, our family, our comforts, and other things.

For Philippine had great dreams and the Revolution seemed to smash them. The Sainte-Marie convent was closed by the government and she had to return home—tried to find another way—even got her own apartment (almost unheard of in those days) in order to carry on her work with the poor and political prisoners of the day. The guillotine was very busy those days. She eventually found a way to get Sainte-Marie back. Then one day some visitors climbed the hill and there was Sophie. At that moment, Sophie Barat and Philippine Duchesne met for the first time. Sophie was twenty-five and Philippine was ten years older. A new type of journey began calling for Philippine to let go, change, and be transformed. A refining of God's zeal was catching fire in her.

Philippine had to let go of her Visitation convent and her beloved grilles and was called to embrace another life that opened up to her in the newly formed Society of the Sacred Heart.

She, at the age of forty-nine, had to let go of her country and the world she had known for the strong pull of God to go to another land and bring God's love there in a new way.

She had to let go of having her ministry among the native tribes and embrace founding schools in the emerging cities along the Mississippi and Missouri Rivers.

She had to let go of educating in a French way and educate the American girls who grew up in a different reality and culture.

She tried to let go of her French and embrace the new language of English and that of the Potawatomi, but she had to give up on that one.

She let go of accomplishing great things herself and became the empty vessel that God's zeal could fill, and she embraced this call in the silence of her heart by being a strong, steady, prayerful presence to her sisters and others, doing what she could, where she could.

I had the privilege of meeting an Indian woman whose great-grandmother was taught by Philippine. She and her friends welcomed us as "Sisters of Philippine." It is amazing to think that Philippine was at the Indian mission only a little over one year, and yet her life has influenced so many generations in Kansas and beyond. She was known as the "woman who always prays."

She had to let go of the dream of bringing the Society beyond the Rockies, but we are here!

And so, in being here, we want to embrace what she gave each of us.

Legend has it that the Indian children put kernels of corn on the hem of her garment to see if she would move during the long hours she prayed. They had no idea of the intimacy she realized with God and the burning desire to bring the kingdom of God to the entire world.

So, we too, in gospel fashion, tonight try to touch the hem of her garment that the power of God's love would touch us and move us to be all that can be in Christ.

Lest you think that Philippine's mission and call of God to this land accomplished nothing, let me state some facts about what happened from the landing of the *Rebecca* to her death in 1852. As Walter Burghardt, SJ, said about Philippine, "She never said it's the Potawatomi or it's no go." Never.

1818   Opened and closed Saint Charles
1819   Florissant
1821   Grand Coteau, Louisiana
1825   Saint Michael in Louisiana
1827   City House in Saint Louis
1828   Re-opened Saint Charles
1841   New York City

1842   McSherrystown in Pennsylvania

1842   Saint Jacques-de-l'Achigan, Canada

1851   Detroit

1851   Baton Rouge, Louisiana

1852   Kenwood, Albany, New York

Think of how long it might take the U.S. Congress to get a satisfactory health care bill passed, and then think of what this valiant woman and her companions accomplished between 1818 and 1852.

Unless the grain of wheat falls to the ground and dies, it remains a single grain. But if it has new life, it yields a rich harvest. As one person has said, "Philippine reminds us that we are not called to be successful, but to be faithful, and to be faith-full is to risk literally all and let God be God." The rich harvest is the mystery of God as it unfolds, and it is seen in unexpected ways and places. Sometimes we are allowed to see what a hundredfold of seed development really looks like.

She stands among us as a mighty oak urging us to risk, to be strong in faith, and creative in action. Above all, to be the Heart of God wherever we are right now, in this place, and in this ever-present moment.

A Prayer Poem to Philippine

Sharon Karam, RSCJ

It is truly right and appropriate
    that you are so starkly honored
    in the annals of the Church, Philippine,
For the example you have left us with is stark and strong,
    and your memory unremittingly ascetical.
But we remember you today
    above all
    for the warmth and light
    which are also part of your heritage.
We remember and celebrate
    the energy, the zeal, the hours of prayer,
    the difficulties with language, the misunderstandings among your own,
    and the undying dedication to your "savages."
We remember the treks across cold Missouri snow,
    we remember the pain of slow mail,
    we remember but do not really understand the months of too little food,
    as well as the months of too much strain.
We call upon you now to renew our hearts again,
    in the land you kissed so lovingly, and sacrificed for so generously.

Renew in us the vision that sends us daily
     to the frontiers of human lives in our care.
Our terrain is better known, but no less challenging;
     our surroundings are amenable, but no less in need of the word of God.
So we thank you for the courage that brought you here on the *Rebecca,*
     and we beg you for the light that will enable us to grow
     in the vision that sends us into this still new world
     with our ciboria, to open new tabernacles in the desert of today,
     and to give flesh to his growing body, straining toward full stature.

Courage, Vision, and Prayer

Marie Louise Schroen, RSCJ
November 16, 1990

ON THIS DAY WE celebrate Saint Philippine's feast and the anniversary of the death of the six Jesuit martyrs and their companions in El Salvador. I would like to reflect for a few moments on the courage of our saint.

"Courage," says Saint Thomas Aquinas, "issues from a holy aggressiveness, a forward movement of the spirit whereby one takes the offensive against dangers, difficulties and labors, undaunted by fear, determined to sweep them from the path and win the goal."

Turning to Philippine, we see this passage of the *Summa* come to life in her courage: courage of initiative, courage of endurance.

Why *courage*? Because under the light of God she had *vision*; vision of the reign of God, which is God present and active freely in his world to save and make use in part of his Son's disciples to do so. A vision of the unobtrusive presence of the mystery of God in mercy; a vision fed by prayer, always prayer, (without me you can do nothing), the courage of initiative in a world of upheaval, the end of an age. The newness of the American frontiers, the needs of the Native Americans, *courage of endurance*: all those years of misunderstanding, physical and, as she believed, failure.

Courage, vision, prayer, what is Philippine to us? A Religious of the Sacred Heart we must honor because she is ours? Or a friend, a guide, a helper in this new age, which, like hers, leaves the past behind in shambles and faces an uncertain dawn?

Mother Duchesne, help us in this hour of need! You, so full of tenderness for your family, we too are your family! You so given to your new country . . . it is our country. Cleanse us of pettiness and greed and fear. Obtain for us the gift of prayer, prayer we need to understand the mystery of the Cross: *not death, but life through death*. We give you the little we have. As the Potawatomi said:

> She learned to weave from us,
> We learned prayer from her face.

A Dream of the Frontier

Mary Schumacher, RSCJ
November 18, 2004

TODAY WE CELEBRATE THE feast of Saint Rose Philippine Duchesne. When I remember her I think of three words: compassion, challenge, contemplation.

She was born in Grenoble, France, in 1769. She grew up in a row house that was situated between two squares: to the left was the political square where her father worked as an attorney (and where the French Revolution actually began in 1788, a year before gaining momentum throughout the country); to the right was the square named Saint Louis. At an early age, after listening to a missionary in school at the Visitation Convent founded by Saint Francis de Sales across the river, she dreamed of becoming a missionary. She entered the convent against the will of her father and shortly had to leave turned out by the Revolution. She ministered with compassion to the poor and the oppressed during the French Revolution. In 1801, she was able to return to the monastery.

Philippine continued to be challenged by her call to become a missionary. In 1804, she met Madeleine Sophie Barat, the founder of the Society of the Sacred Heart, ten years younger than she. Bishop Dubourg of Saint Louis, Missouri, visited the motherhouse in Paris, and Philippine begged to be sent to evangelize the Native Americans. In 1818, she came along with four other religious to Saint Louis. She founded the first free school west of the Mississippi River at age forty-nine. Within fifteen years, fifty women joined her in religious life. As the first missionary of our community, she began the spread of the love of the Sacred Heart of Jesus across the world.

Finally, when I think of Philippine, I think of the word contemplation. At the age of seventy-two, her dream of evangelizing the Native Americans was fulfilled. She journeyed to the Potawatomi Indians in Kansas in 1842. Legend has it that the Indians used to put corn on her habit while she was praying and discovered that she never moved throughout the night in front of the Blessed Sacrament. As a result they came to call her "The Woman Who Prays Always."

So what can we learn from her life of sacrifice of country, the challenge of living on the frontier of the Wild West when she arrived in the United States, and her time with the native Americans? The Church canonized her as the fifth American saint on July 3, 1988. She is one of our heroes from whom we can learn the value of living with compassion, following the challenge of our personal call, and contemplation, to be in union with the love of the Sacred Heart of Jesus as we live each day. A saying I often reflect on is "Keep your dreams alive as reality stretches out to meet them." Philippine did just that. She never lost her vision and dream, even in the midst of feeling a failure oftentimes, and her reality came true for her at the age of seventy-two. She died on November 18, 1852, and so we celebrate her life and her love for God and others today.

What are the frontiers in our life today?

Blessed Rose Philippine Duchesne

John Courtney Murray, SJ
1940

IT IS SURELY NO accident that God should have chosen this particular moment in the history of our country and of the world to declare to us through his Church that Philippine Duchesne is Blessed with him in heaven. Her blessedness means above all that she shares in heaven in the redemptive power of his glorified Son, Jesus Christ, and hence it gives to us the blessed certainty that she is our strong ally in our work for the Kingdom of his Son on earth.

We need that certainty. Our work is to live the life of a child of God, a member of Christ, an instrument of the Holy Spirit for humanity's salvation. And there is one supreme virtue that we need above all if we are to live such a life in this day and age. I mean the virtue of fortitude, "strongness," courage.

God has seen our need. and his fatherly Providence has provided for it by the Beatification of Philippine Duchesne. For thereby he has given us, I think, a sign of his will that we pattern our souls on the heroic model of hers. And more than that, he has given us the certainty that he has ready for us, through her intercession, the gift that he gave to her, the gift of an irresistible thrusting, an imperturbably calm, an unbreakably constant courage.

Today then I would briefly sketch this outstanding quality of hers, and speak too of our need of it.

It is no mere conceit to say that Saint Thomas Aquinas, were he to have seen the life of Philippine Duchesne as it unrolled, would have found in it the materials and the model for the superb description of the virtue of fortitude that he wrote in the *Secunda-Secundae*.

Courage, he says, is "steadiness of soul." It is first a "general virtue, or rather the condition of all virtue, for (as Aristotle taught ...) virtue is a matter of steady and unfaltering action," that is, courageous action. It is moreover a special virtue, which imparts to the soul a particular power, a power of steadiness in the face of fear. The action of fear on the human soul is shaking, shattering, destructive of all virtue; and to stand firm against it one needs the virtue of courage.

Then, analyzing further the steadiness of soul in the face of fear, he describes how it shows itself in a two-fold act, each of which demands for its perfection two subsidiary virtues.

Courage, he says, issues first in a holy aggressiveness, a forward movement of the soul whereby we take the offensive against dangers and difficulties and labors, undaunted by fear of them, determined to sweep them from our path and win through our goal.

And this courage of initiative is supported first by the virtue of confidence. Confidence gives a readiness and springiness to the soul, keying it up for the plunge into conflict by filling it with the hope of great achievements and the certainty of victory over obstacles. Secondly, the courage of initiative is supported by the virtue of magnificence. Magnificence means a splendid disregard of the cost involved in carrying through high resolves and swooping plans. It implies a certain strenuousness of soul, a willingness to spare no effort or expense in the achievement of success.

Aggressiveness, however, is not the highest act of courage. Under the impulse of enthusiasm one can at times move high-heartedly into the fight; but to stay in it when the blows are actually falling, that demands a steadier soul. And so, higher than the courage of initiative is the courage of endurance; the steadiness of soul whereby one "stands unfalteringly in the midst of dangers," and refuses to crack under the pressure of the tasks undertaken.

And this courage of endurance calls for two subsidiary virtues. The first is the virtue of patience. Under the pressure of work or difficulty the soul has a tendency to sag, or better, to disintegrate, to lose its "wholeness." It hesitates, grows anxious, depressed, unsure. Its vision of its own objective comes unfocused; it loses its grip on its own resolve; even physical and nervous resources are drained. Sadness (to use St. Thomas' generic term) invades it. And against the disintegrating action of sadness, that most insidious enemy of sustained effort, the soul must stand firm by the virtue of patience. Patience keeps the soul serene and whole, and thus fortifies its endurance.

The second aspect of the courage of endurance is the virtue of perseverance. Really, it is the decisive virtue that gives to courage its perfection, namely, its lastingness. It does indeed take courage to set one's foot on arduous slopes and begin the ascent; but to follow the road though it wind uphill all the way, that is the supreme test of courage. One can endure for a while, but being human one grows weary of enduring. Sheer time saps vital energy; he or she longs to pause, turn off, turn back, give up. And against the undermining action of time and weariness stands the virtue of perseverance. Perseverance means constancy in courage. And only through constancy can courage win its victory.

This, in brief and inadequate outline, is Saint Thomas's description of the virtue of courage; it is a confident and magnificent, a patient and persevering steadiness of soul in the face of danger and difficulty, and the fear they naturally inspire in the soul.

Now, if you turn from the sober pages of the *Summa* to the biography of Blessed Philippine Duchesne, you will see Saint Thomas's academic description suddenly take life before you, become incarnate by the power of the Holy Spirit in the history of a human soul. What he wrote, she lived.

How splendidly she lived it! Her life is a series of courageous initiatives, a tale of courageous endurance. For both these acts of courage God had equipped her nature, and dwelling in her by grace he brought his natural gifts to towering perfection.

Perhaps in her earlier years it is her courage of initiative that is rather more salient. Many instances illustrate it, but to me a typical one is her bold attempt to restore the Visitation convent of Sainte-Marie-d'En-Haut, dispersed by the Revolution of 1791. I think of her on that bleak December night in 1801 when alone save for one girl-companion she took possession of her former school and home, which ten years of desecration and neglect had reduced to rack and ruin.

That was indeed an act of holy aggressiveness. She had already found a sphere of usefulness and a way to sanctity in the care of the neglected children of Grenoble. But its horizons were too small for her great soul. So forward she moved, to extend them. From what was good she went on to what was great; characteristically first in the field, she aspired to restore to Dauphiny religious life in community, and thus stem the wasting pestilence of secularism by sending forth new streams of Christian sanctity and culture.

There is a startling confidence in that forward move, for the odds against her seemed insuperable. But it was not in herself she trusted, but in the power of God, who had inspired her initiative.

There is, too, magnificence in the move. Perhaps not the magnificence of a mind that can plan great things and organize their execution (I have never persuaded myself that she had the gifts of a great administrator), but rather the magnificence of a heart that can dare great things in the assurance that God has somehow planned them and will see them through, provided men do not hang back timidly.

You can see her type of magnificence, I think in her characteristic reply to the ever-prudent Père Varin on the occasion of his visit of inspection to Sainte-Marie. Her ardent desire was for union with the Sacred Heart foundation already made at Amiens, but all she could get out of him was something about "the slowness of God's ways." "Surely not," she burst out, "do not the Scriptures speak of him as a giant running his course?"

That was her youthful idea of God. She felt that he knew whither he was going; she felt, too, the impelling power of his inspiration. Why then delay? Why wait for maps and surveys, careful estimates of cost? When God runs, shall man walk?

So she reasoned then. And at the moment she was right, and she won her point. But she did not yet know all of God's gifts. It required long years and the gentle genius of Madeleine Sophie Barat to teach her that God can likewise walk, and most often does.

And Philippine Duchesne, who despised parochial limits, if imposed by timidity on her efforts towards sanctity and on her apostolic work, learned to love them when they were imposed by obedience.

It was a hard lesson. True, she had a supremely gifted teacher, a woman of courage equal to her own, but of wider vision and of unique genius for government. But still the lesson was a trying one. To Philippine Duchesne it came hard to walk, to wait, to submit her springing spirit of initiative to the curb of a superior's will.

Inevitably then those fourteen years in Europe after her entrance into the Society of the Sacred Heart were testing, educative years. As you know, she longed to launch herself on a venture dreamed of since her girlhood visit to the tomb of Saint Francis Regis—the missions in America. Constantly the desire to be off consumed her interiorly. But as she had the courage to act without a word, she likewise had the courage to wait for the word to act.

At last it came, in 1818. She was forty-eight years old—the age, one would say, whose ideal is security, not adventure, comfortable consolations, not perilous initiatives. But her youthful spirit still lived strongly in her. The years had tempered it, but in the firm and gentle hands of Saint Madeleine Sophie it had lost none of its tensile strength. It vaulted her across the seas, into a land of which she knew only one thing, that it had been given by the Father to his Incarnate Son as part of his inheritance, and that it was her privilege and duty to bring it under the loving dominion of his royal Heart.

The departure for America was the supreme act of her courage of initiative, and it ushered in the final period of her life, wherein God tested his child's courage of endurance, and by his unconquerable grace gave her the victory.

You know the history of those thirty-four years in Midwestern America, and the heroic steadiness of soul that they demanded of her. I myself have never read the story of them without a feeling of awe.

Awe, first of all, at her patience, the indomitable, serene, even gay courage with which she bore every imaginable hardship. Of all the blows that life can aim at body and soul to break them, not a single one was spared her.

There was the hardship of a poverty truly appalling, the deprivation of the very necessities of life, in the midst of surroundings utterly comfortless. Poverty can be a soul-cramping thing, but it only served to widen her great soul; out of her store of almost nothing, she fed and clothed my own brothers in their early days in Missouri. For that she will always live, tenderly loved, in Jesuit memories.

There was the hardship of frequent, often serious illness. Illness can break up a soul, turn it in upon itself, and paralyze its power of devotion. But for her it was wholly sanctifying, a new way opened into the deepest recesses of the pierced Heart of Christ.

Severer than the physical burdens that gradually broke her iron constitution were the blows that fell upon her soul. I shall not speak of the blow of disillusionment at finding the country and the work so very different from what she had expected. (The Indians, for instance, when at last she saw them, were by no means the noble savages of Jean-Jacques Rousseau.) Disillusionment is always the missionary's great temptation; it lurks in the path of greatly zealous souls who go out to set the world on fire and find that it does not kindle quickly enough. She felt the temptation, but shook it off. For hers was not the superficial type of soul for whom it is disastrous.

Moreover, I cannot pause to detail the rain of blows that fell, not on herself directly but on her work, and were consequently all the more rocking. I mean the seemingly endless delays in beginning, the constant check that circumstances put on all her desires and plans, the overwhelming odds piled up against every venture, the threat of insecurity that menaced each of them, the calamities that not infrequently swept away what had been laboriously set afoot.

I would speak rather of two trials of her patient steadiness that seem to me to bring her closer to ourselves.

The first is the fact that all of her life she was in the heart-breaking situation of the competent workman compelled to do his work without proper tools, and consequently compelled to see his products come from his hands misshapen and unfinished. She had to found convents in surroundings unfit for community life, where even the services of a priest were often lacking. She had to start schools where even books were lacking for the pupils. She never had enough nuns to staff the schools founded, never enough money for necessary improvements and expansion, never enough of anything. Never had she the joy of offering to God a work that fulfilled her own ideal of what was worthy of him.

It was a desperately discouraging situation. Doubtless, none of us has been immersed in it so deeply as she was. But we have all perhaps felt the dismay inspired by the lack of things we seemingly need for the work that we are called to do, whatever it be. And we have felt, too, the inevitable temptation either to throw aside our inadequate tools and give up, or else to use them half-heartedly and be content with mediocre performance.

But the inexhaustible patience of Philippine Duchesne could yield to no such temptation. By the power of patient faith she stayed steadfastly at her discouraging tasks. She knew what we must learn, that the proper tools for any of God's work are those his Providence puts into our hands, and that if only we use them to the full our handiwork will be perfect in his sight.

The second trial of her patience was the severest of all. Not only did she feel the lack of proper tools for her work, but for years the conviction grew in her that she was not herself the proper tool.

There is no doubt that she considered herself a failure, in all her undertakings, and especially in her office as superior. We know it as humility, but to her it was a simple truth. And a terribly bitter truth. I cannot think that she found it easy to accept failure. Both her natural character and her intense zeal for the glory of the Sacred Heart must have fought the very idea of it. And I am sure that God could have asked of her no greater proof of patient courage than the willingness to go on for years at a work for which she was intimately convinced she was not fit.

We, of course, know that she was the grain of wheat destined to fall into the ground and die, that of it a rich harvest might come. But she herself had no vision of the future. Her own eyes did not view the harvest, the Society of the Sacred Heart in America, nor did her heart have the joy of knowing that its every member, Mother or Sister, would be what she so greatly desired: *"bien de la race,"* as Bishop Dubourg said of her first community at Florissant. She did indeed look upon the first-fruits of her sacrifice, the first vocations in America. They were her single, but very great joy, for she saw in them ardor and courage and self-spending generosity—all the qualities she loved.

But for the rest, she was subject to the same law as we: she did not know the value of her own work. She looked at it as clearly as she could and judged it nothing worth. Yet she went on doing it, sustained only by her patient faith in the God of Abraham, "who giveth life from the dead and nameth the things that are not as though they were" (Romans 4:17).

And therein at least we can claim a likeness to her. There is no intelligent man or woman, gifted with any sense of earnestness, who has not at some time, and perhaps often, felt that depressing sense of inadequacy before some task or ideal, or who has not measured achievements with desires and had the conviction of failure. There is no experience so apt to take the heart out of one.

But it did not take the heart out of Philippine Duchesne. Rather it put a heart into her, the heart of Christ, patiently obedient unto death, even to the death of the Cross. In deepest union with the patient Heart she went on.

She went on and on. That was, I think, the ultimate triumph of her superb courage: not her triumph over hardship, but her triumph over time.

Time is the agent of change, and hence the insidious, implacable enemy of each one's high resolves, hopes, and loves. From its tearing claws nothing is safe, save God, the Unchanging Good. She fears time. Continually she prays that it may not vanquish us and make us change with its changing. Insistently, incessantly, she begs of God for her children the grace of constancy, the gift of perseverance, whereby they may stand firm to the end.

It is my own favorite thought of Philippine Duchesne: her glorious conquest of time. God let it spare her none of its ravages. He let it rob her of all the things on this earth that once she loved. It robbed her of physical energy and reduced her to helplessness. It robbed her of her sense of active usefulness, pushed her aside to a corner to watch while others carried on. It robbed her of the fruits of her work, bringing changing circumstances that undermined all she had tried to do. It robbed her of every bright dream of achievement that once she cherished. Bitterest theft of all, it robbed her of her friends, those loving friends and loyal allies who had stood with her in her trials, with whom she had labored and suffered, whom she had guided and leaned on and loved. Then for two long years it robbed her of her only human support, communion by letter with the great soul in France with whom her own soul was bound by ties of tenderest intimacy. And in place of all the things it took from her, time left her only loneliness, the isolation of age that lives in the past, left behind, while the life of the world presses remorselessly on to the future.

Yet against the lonely citadel wherein her spirit dwelt, time hurled its assaults in vain. Against the steadiness of her unwearying courage, they shattered harmlessly. Indeed she not only stood off time's attacks, she overthrew the enemy and made it her ally. Because her soul was deep and strong, time, the ravager, enriched her.

She watched it change all things about her and only grew more serene in patience. Gladly she let go the things it took from her, for in their going they enriched her with one infinitely peaceful conviction, from which she drew the strength for unswerving constancy in love and sacrifice. From time's changing she learned that God abides, and that his Son, Christ Jesus, is Priest unchangeably after the manner of Melchisedech. She learned that only one human act has ever proved eternal, the Sacrifice of Christ, offered on Calvary and offered eternally in heaven, where the Victim of man's inconstancy stands with his Wounds in the sight of the Father, "forever living to make intercession for us." And consequently, she learned that only those human things are rescued from time's destruction that have been laid on the altar of the passing minute in union with the Sacrifice of Christ, and thus through him have passed into God's immutable possession.

Thus time led her, as it should lead each one of us, ever more deeply into the mystery of the Cross, the sign of victory, planted in time and enduring eternally. In union with Christ Crucified she conquered.

And now she reigns in heaven with the Victor-King who gave her victory. So the Church has told us, that we ourselves may take heart, and be steadied by new hope of victory. For we know that Philippine Duchesne loves America; from it she suffered, and for it she suffered. We know that she wills the sanctification of America. And so we may have the blessed certainty that in our efforts towards sanctity God will give us through her the grace to be, as she was, unconquerable.

Philippine Duchesne: Woman of Graced Stamina

Barbara Quinn, RSCJ
Catholic Theological Union
November 18, 1997

RECENTLY I READ KATHLEEN NORRIS' *The Cloister Walk*. Her entry for November 1-2 reads: *"Photismos"* is a word I've learned today, from Father Godfrey, an ancient word for baptism. I like the way it shares a root with photosynthesis, the way the saints might be said to have heeded the command of 1 John 3, to "come to the light" (47).

The saints' photosynthesis, the mysterious creation of essential life-bearing elements when one meets and mingles with the Son through baptism, leads us into a reflection about today's saint, Rose Philippine Duchesne. This French woman brought the Society of the Sacred Heart to the American frontier only eighteen years after its founding in 1800. She planted a seed of oak, as the name Duchesne suggests, that continues to grow not only here in the United States but in more than forty countries around the world.

Before turning to the flowering of her labors, however, let us consider for a moment the seeds and bulbs that lie buried in our quickly freezing yards of Chicago's Hyde Park. I lament the passing of the beautiful flowers that carpeted our lawn not long ago. Only faith and experience tell us that they will appear again, as we feel the cold and hear the crunch of our feet on the frost laden leaves and imagine the dark and deadly crust that houses the seed and bulbs now.

Philippine's life was often like this season. Although she had some flowering achievements, Philippine more often than not felt the cold failure. So why is she a saint? She is a saint, I believe, because this oak seed, frequently buried in darkness, was dogged in her search for the Light of God, which she believed reached persistently into her world on a mission of love. It is precisely this aspect of her saintliness that offers us great hope and joy.

I don't know how she did it, except that baptismal photosynthesis produced in her a *graced stamina* that allowed her to keep turning towards the Light of Life. Examples abound but a few snapshots of her life will serve the point.

Philippine was known to grow attached to people and places and familiar modes of life like the cloister grilles that Madeleine Sophie insisted be removed, yet Philippine begged to leave all things familiar in order to journey to the New World so that the "savages" could also hear the glad and hopeful tidings of the gospel.

When she received permission to embark on this mission after years of waiting, Philippine was elated. But her elation was soon drowned in the storm-tossed sea of her own heart, as she experienced a surprising but unrelenting and tumultuous desolation that began during her retreat prior to leaving France and continued throughout the seventy-two-day voyage to America. Her soul, she said, was "in a state of anguish, hard and dark."

Although the darkness lifted as they arrived on the marshy ground of New Orleans, the darkness was never far from her. She was named what was comparable to provincial though she felt neither the inclination nor the ability to do the job. But Philippine forged ahead toward the light, establishing schools, weathering the storms of criticism from her own sisters, negotiating with bishop and businessperson for property and money, knowing often enough they were taking advantage of her and her sisters. She spoke with candor about wrongs committed. She pleaded to be released from her position of authority. But always, with dogged determination, she held to the mission she had come for, sometimes with standards that seemed too much for her companions: her unwavering commitment to the poor and her unflinching insistence that the sisters, too, live simply in order to share the life of the people and the Christ who had called them there.

Her lifelong desire to work with the Indians, which really fueled her desire to go to America in the first place, was realized only at seventy-one when she journeyed to Sugar Creek, Kansas, to work among the Potawatomi Indians. The work of this very frail old lady was only one: to pray. The Indians, whose language she could never learn, understood her goodness through the darkness of no words. They simply wanted to be around her, and gently touch her garments so that they could "take grace." Many blessings she had indeed but the struggle of the seed dying was likewise a constant companion.

This member of the communion of saints, I believe, has something to say to us whether RSCJ or not. Philippine reveals the hidden work of God that goes on in the ordinary and sometimes very dark moments of our lives. But she persisted in her belief that the Spirit of God moved within her and around her, prompting her forward, turning the eyes of her heart with a graced stamina to seek the traces of God's light, living now no longer for herself alone but for the One who reaches out to us in love and who asks us to share that mission.

Sometimes I don't know how we face the dark moments either, the dying seeds, the hidden journey. Seeking the Light with graced stamina for the long haul is tough and truly requires a saintly vigor . . .

the long haul of study where our desire to know can surprise us in an unknowing that is born of God but that is demanding;

the unrelenting battle against suffering and illness that we must fight until there is nothing more to be done but to surrender to it;

the arduous crossing of the seas of racial, economic, religious, and cultural differences and even hatreds in the hope of bridging our disparate worlds;

the unending commitment to renew a Church that is meant to stand as a beacon of hope for people everywhere, including those within;

the life long journey of our heart's conversions to become simple and supple enough to die to anything that obstructs the Light of the Spirit, even in the daily duties that can sometimes weigh us down as much as major crises can.

Perhaps it is especially in the struggle to seek the Light, forcing us to push to the new, the "More," that we break out of our darkened, encrusted egos to burst or crawl towards the light of God's freedom and love, no longer for ourselves but for those who need God's love and mercy.

And so we come to this table, in the company of the saints like Philippine who urge us forward, reminding us that Christ's "hour," our hour, is passion and glory intertwined, alternating darkness and light, blood and water, death and life intermingled. The flowers will indeed appear again someday. Let us pray today for Philippine's graced stamina to turn towards the Light as we wait.

Philippine as Our Guide

On Reclaiming the Past: RSCJ and Philippine Duchesne

Carol Purtle
Feast of Blessed Philippine, 1985

MANY OF US HAVE a rather simplified view of Philippine: she was a strong person, suffered a great deal, and was hard on herself in a way we're not prepared to be. For whatever reason, our associations with wormwood, frozen rivers, and closets under the stairs have permitted many of us to niche Philippine in the shadowy past and revive her memory with different levels of enthusiasm only once a year.

While I don't want to appear a total revisionist, I do think that we need to update our prejudices about Philippine, if only to allow ourselves once again the inspiration of one of the two RSCJ to have been clearly honored by the official Church. As her religious descendants in this country, we owe our founding pioneer at least another look.

The perspective I have chosen for this reflection deals with our life today as much as it does with hers in the early nineteenth century. It concerns categories of vocation, ministry, spirituality, and her personal response to situations of daily life that we all face, and which she faced with characteristic vigor. I apologize for asking you to bear with the jargon of the present rather than with the more familiar categories of the past.

First, to set the stage in terms of spirituality and vocation, Philippine was the first major transfer candidate to the Society. Her Visitandine background in Grenoble no doubt prepared her for the life she was to lead in the Society, but her basic spirituality remained clearly distinct from that of Madeleine Sophie. From the beginning of her experience with the Society, then, she had to follow her initial inspiration as well as willingly adapt and embrace the spirit of another way.

In 1818, one of the tasks facing the Society's leadership was the problem of developing a ministry plan—or of finding a way to answer the call to developing ministries in new areas when personnel and resources were limited. In discerning her ministry within this framework, Philippine would certainly not be considered an ideal model of behavior by present standards. With regard to her desire to serve in the New World, she maintained little sense of spiritual, physical, or emotional indifference; further, she managed to have the Church hierarchy (in the person of Bishop Dubourg) pressure the Society into also wanting what she wanted. (Note: I do not wish to take a position about which elements in her life are to be considered an inspiration. I'm simply saying that the thought of her name on the register of the beatified might be a help to us!)

Once her call to the New World was confirmed by the fact that the Society sent her to Bishop Dubourg in the Louisiana territory, her missionary vision of work among the Indians was dashed by his practical direction to do what he thought was most needed. Instead of Indians, it was to be settlers; instead of following her spiritual vision, she was to open schools. Instead of Saint Louis, it was to be Saint Charles, and so forth. All these developments are well known to us. Having used the Church hierarchy to affirm her calling, she now found she had little control as to how that calling would be defined in location and service.

Most people who read the plaque at the Missouri Historical Society and find that she opened the first free school for girls west of the Mississippi would never dream that she would rather have been doing something else, like living among the Native Americans. The Society's educational mission thus took a historic step forward with Philippine, but we rarely reflect on the power of this educational initiative for the direction of the Society's identity, and we rarely discuss Philippine when we trace the history of the Society's educational mission.

The years of her full activity were spent between her arrival on these shores in 1818 and the realization of her spiritual call to the Potawatomi of Kansas twenty-three years later. When we read the letters of those years, fraught as they are with pioneering activities we now recognize as "historic"—the founding of schools, the securing of houses for the Society in Louisiana and Missouri, the labors she undertook in places where we no longer have houses—we need to look as well at the attitudes that do not go down as "historic." Among these are certainly her attitudes toward cloister, toward separation from figures of Society authority, and toward her own spiritual and mental health. Though the concept and fact of cloister helped establish the sense of place by which the Society still tends to think of itself, Philippine's emphasis was more on the sense of interdependence that life on the frontier required than on any sense of separation or privilege the concept could later have afforded.

We all remember how often her letters to France expressed sentiments such as "It is impossible to tell you what it is like here; it is not at all like France." That "not at all like France" also covered the many differences from Louisiana to Missouri to Kansas and so forth. She had no home visit to look forward to, no sense that she would ever see France again, and no steady reliable communication with Society authority.

In our more recent attempts to define our internationality and centralize our authority structure, we can probably identify a little more than formerly with this aspect of her life. Where we live as individuals and where and how we connect personally with authority figures still make a great deal of difference to individuals and authority figures alike. To live even in a different community, not to mention a different city, state, or region of the country, is to take both a personal and a communal risk in today's Society. We tend to think these things didn't matter much to Philippine; once she had left France, she understood what it was to leave everything. If these things matter in such an extreme way today—which authority figures visit us, how our personal relationships with them are defined, how we are affirmed in ministry—certainly we are not able to say those issues meant nothing to people of another age, even though they appeared truly given to the love of God!

Up to now, however, the image of Philippine's daily life is still one of hardship, suffering, and forbearance. It will never change totally, but it could be important for us to reflect on her attitude as she faced daily tasks. By today's methods of determining personality, interest, and aptitude, she would probably not have come out high on leadership, humor, public speaking, diplomacy, gift for languages, or interest in travel. Persuasion would probably have been high, but there appeared to be little developed capacity to cope with stress except prayer and personal penance. Her illness of 1840 would certainly have to be categorized as some type of psychic depression. Even in the early days, she would hardly have survived the screening process for potentially stable missionaries.

In spite of what hindsight tells us were extreme difficulties, however, we do not find much regret in her daily life. She is never simply biding time until she gets a job doing what she is really called to do! No group has examined her milieu and affirmed its suitability to the Society's mission; she was rarely affirmed in her leadership, intellectual prowess, or balanced judgment. Even after many years, she was hardly considered "representative" of the American mission. If she had been subject to our system of governance, she would probably never have been elected to a committee, let alone a representative assembly or general chapter. Yet the people she served, both within and without the Society, never felt that she was less than totally given to the task at hand. The fact that she was not perfectly gifted for all dimensions of her ministry did not prevent her from doing her best every day.

One element enlivened her daily routine, however, and kept her devoted to the many undertakings for which we would probably declare her unsuited. The Potawatomi summed it up in the title: "Woman who prays always."

The bronze plaque honoring her among other pioneer women at the Jefferson Memorial in Saint Louis reminds us that "some names must not wither." Today we are sometimes found characterizing ourselves as pioneer women in a new age and a new context. Our roles are changing, and little is turning out as we might have expected. In the many circumstances of this new age (to which we might actually find ourselves ill-suited by gift and temperament), we should certainly not attempt to go forward without every bit of inspiration to which we are entitled. We may readily find solace and insight in the daily life and example of that very ordinary person who began the Society's work on these shores. Indeed, some names must not wither in our memory or in our tradition. Among these is certainly that of Rose Philippine Duchesne, who bore a title with which we can all identify and to which each one must equally aspire; not that of *Beata* or "founding pioneer," but one that marked her spiritual character, daily life, and religious identity as it must mark ours, namely that given her by the Potawatomi: "woman who prays always."

God's Plan

Archbishop Thomas Wenski
Carrollton School of the Sacred Heart
November 20, 2012

I HOPE THAT ALL of you know something about Saint Rose Philippine Duchesne. Today is her feast day—she was a saint, a holy woman, and a Religious of the Sacred Heart—in fact, she came from France along with some other sisters of the Sacred Heart to open up schools on the frontier in the early nineteenth century. And it is no exaggeration to say that Carrollton would not be here today if Saint Rose Philippine and her sisters hadn't come to America to start those first schools.

So today we remember a woman of faith—and a woman of action but also a woman of prayer.

Even though she was born in France, she ended up on America's frontier; even though she had a hard time learning English, she taught children of settlers in Missouri. And even though at seventy-two she was already weak because of sickness, she went to work among the Native Americans. What a life's journey she had! Full of challenges—overcoming persecution as a child in her own country because she was a believer, building schools with little resources, teaching children in a language other than her native French, suffering failing health and yet keeping up a hectic schedule and seeming to be always praying.

As you look where life took Philippine, I'd ask you to ask yourselves: where is your life going to take you? Because you are young, most of your life's journey still lies before you. Because you are Americans "you are offered many opportunities for personal development, and you are brought up with a sense of generosity, service and fairness." But "there are also difficulties: activities and mindsets that stifle hope, pathways that seem to lead to happiness and fulfillment but in fact end only in confusion and fear." (Cf. Pope Benedict XVI to young people, New York, 2008.)

Being a Catholic Christian—for Rose Philippine Duchesne and for each one of us—means simply to commit ourselves to walk in the Lord's footsteps even when our path takes us through twists and turns, through the joys and trials of ordinary life. With the Holy Spirit to strengthen and guide us along the way, our own lives then become a journey of hope.

What are your plans? What do you want to do with your life? What do you want to be when you grow up? Well, today, I would ask you to consider this question from a different perspective. Instead of asking, what are my plans; what do I want to do; ask instead: What is God's plan for my life? What does God want me to do with my life?

What is God's plan for your life? God does have a plan for each one of us—for in God's eyes, no one is an accident. "Each of us is the result of a thought of God. Each of us is willed, each of us is loved, each of us is necessary" (Pope Benedict, 4/24/05). We find a general outline of God's plan for us in Jesus' words to his disciples: "Just as I have loved you, you also should love one another" (John 13:34). God calls each one of us to a future of love. To give your very self as a gift to God and to your brothers and sisters, as Jesus did when he died for us on the cross, is the way to true joy and happiness. This is not an easy way; but it is the way, God's way.

Dare, then, to love as Christ loves. Loving in this way is like learning to speak a new language well, or play a new sport.

Before you can speak a new language well, you have to learn the grammar. Grammar might seem to be all about rules and regulations. And to love like Jesus means learning the rules and regulations about self-control, purity of heart and mind; it is about learning how to deny oneself, to respect others, to serve instead of being served. And as you learn the grammar, you have to practice, practice, practice . . .

It's the same way in learning a new sport. We all have celebrated that Lebron James has signed with the Miami Heat (and you know he played high school basketball at a Catholic high school). He could perhaps be one of the greatest basketball players of all times. (At least we hope so!) But that does not mean that he can ignore the rules and regulations of basketball. In fact, knowing and keeping the rules make it easier, not harder, to play the game. In the same way, the Commandments, the rules and regulations of Christian living, give us the freedom to embrace a future of love.

Just as a Lebron James can teach us about the game of basketball, the saints can teach us about how to love as Jesus did. We might not all be basketball stars, but we are called "to be holy"; we are called to "fellowship" with Jesus Christ. In other words, we are called to be the best version of ourselves, that version of ourselves that God wants us to be.

In the lives of the saints, we find remarkable journeys of hope: they trusted God, confident that he was their final destination; and each one—in different ways to be sure—but each one offered an outstretched hand of hope to those they met along the way. But as they made their life's journey, Jesus was their constant companion; and they constantly conversed with him along the way.

Obeying the commandments—with the help of God's grace through constant prayer—makes love possible and makes life an exciting adventure as it was for Saint Rose Philippine Duchesne. Her life teaches us that what counts in life is not worldly success but faithfulness to who we are as children of God.

God's plan is for us to love as Jesus did. To work out the details, to learn how God wishes you to shape the future, to overcome one's own hesitancy or fears, requires the same discipline needed to excel in a language or a sport. It also requires that you spend some time talking and listening to Jesus as he walks with you along your way. Perhaps, God has a project of love for your future as a wife or mother. But, at the same time, be ready to say "yes" if the project is to follow the path of consecrated life as did Mother Duchesne—or Sister Cooke.

Where is your life going to take you? Wherever life may lead you, to whatever walk of life, to whatever career or vocational choice, resolve to be like Rose Philippine Duchesne, a woman of faith, a woman of action—and a woman of prayer.

Advice from Philippine

Jeanne Lagrelle, RSCJ

IF I WERE TO have a dialogue with Philippine today, I think she would tell me these four things:

1. Do not forget that prolonged prayer is indispensable, whatever the amount of work, and that sacramental life is my nourishment.

2. No task is contemptible; I must not be afraid of suffering; our encounter with God is realized in everything, as the whole of life is prayer.

3. That I need not worry about small material details; joy must remain if I lack something; the desire and will to bring the Good News to others has been given me by God and can overcome every obstacle.

4. One person sows and another reaps. I take part in salvation by what I am and by what God does through me.

Sanctity and Slavery: A Journey with Philippine Duchesne

Catherine M. Mooney

ALTHOUGH I HAVE NEVER met Philippine Duchesne, who lived some two centuries ago, I find that my relationship with her evinces a few of the features of long term relationships that I share with friends today. For significant periods, most relationships stay pretty much on the same course. Every now and then, however, a bump in the road, a new event, an unexpected revelation, disturbs that steady state and a fresh course is set. Newly calibrated, a relationship is hopefully fine-tuned and strengthened for the next leg of the journey.

Today I feel the ground shifting again as I try to absorb new information about Philippine's involvement in the institution of slavery. The Religious of the Sacred Heart have been plumbing their slaveholding past to better understand it, locate the descendants of people enslaved on their properties, and, especially, address the ongoing evils of racism today.[28] They have also just published the first edition of all of Philippine's writings, making available letters and documents neither I nor most people have ever had a chance to read.[29] A saint and a slaveholder: Philippine is both. Struggling to appreciate each of these identities (Philippine has many more, of course) is an ongoing challenge. It has called me, a white woman, to reflect more deeply about both sanctity and slavery.

Phase 1: I have admired Philippine Duchesne ever since I first heard stories about her forty years ago. These were the stories of a hero. A highborn French woman who gave up a magnificently comfortable life to become a cloistered Visitation nun. A brave stalwart who, after being run out of that monastery by the French Revolution, stealthily made her way through the streets of Grenoble to help priests in hiding and shepherd them to the destitute and dying. When she eventually returned to religious life, now as a Religious of the Sacred

---

28 E.g., Terry L. Jones, "Society of the Sacred Heart Hopes for Understanding, Reconciliation as It Delves into Its History of Slave Ownership," *The Advocate* (March 11, 2018) highlights the research of Maureen Chicoine, RSCJ. The historian Emory C. Webre's research and collaboration are importantly advancing this work.
29 *Philippine Duchesne, pionnière à la frontière américaine: Œuvres complètes (1769-1852)*, ed. Marie-France Carreel, RSCJ, and Carolyn Osiek, RSCJ (Brepols, 2017); English translation forthcoming.

Heart, Philippine was the persistent voice prodding Sophie Barat to extend the Society of the Sacred Heart's mission beyond the well-known contours of Europe.

The Philippine I knew then was the preeminent pioneer, crossing boundaries of class, country, and continent to meet peoples unlike herself in the frontier cultures of the "New" World. She opened the first tuition-free school for girls west of the Mississippi. She founded another school for indigenous girls when virtually no one valued them, much less wanted to teach them. Making her way as a pioneer in relatively rough circumstances, Philippine and her sisters hung laundry in frigid Missouri winters, hauled water, and cared for their cows and other animals. As a nineteenth-century nun, she had to answer to a number of clerical superiors. Collaborating with the best of them, she founded and managed a network of diverse institutions for girls extending from Missouri down to Louisiana along the Mississippi River. But she knew too how to stand up to domineering clerics who proved difficult.

Some of Philippine's admiring contemporaries confirmed this grand image. When she died in 1852, for example, one of her religious sisters remarked that many people thought the world had lost a saint. A Jesuit close to her even mentioned a possible canonization.

This was the first Philippine I met—Philippine the superstar hero. I had come to know her mostly through word-of-mouth, stories passed around and a few light lectures here and there.

Phase 2. When Philippine was eventually canonized in 1988, I wanted both to learn more for myself and to take advantage of that momentous occasion to let others newly interested in "Saint" Philippine learn more about her in a book I was writing.[30]

As I read selected writings by and about her, my relationship with Philippine took a new turn. The strong woman who always stood up to difficult clerics, I learned, sometimes obediently submitted to their harsh treatment. I had earlier known that Philippine could be hard on herself, but reading her writings revealed how exaggeratedly self-blaming she could be. Some of the hero-shine was dimming.

Details regarding her interactions with indigenous people and other people of color was also tarnishing my image. The school Philippine founded for indigenous girls just seven years after arriving in North America turned out to be less than a smashing success. The U.S. government running indigenous peoples off their lands bore much of the blame for the school's failure. But I learned that Philippine would have been happy if the indigenous parents simply left their children behind with the religious. She shared the assumption of other European-descent missionaries that indigenous children could be better educated apart from the influence of their parents. More troubling yet to digest was new knowledge

---

30 *Philippine Duchesne: A Woman with the Poor* (Paulist, 1990; reprinted, Wipf & Stock, 2007).

that the Society of the Sacred Heart owned persons who had been enslaved, some given to them, others purchased. Philippine's involvement was not fully clear to me—she resided in Missouri and most of the enslaved persons were in the convents in the South, where slavery was more widespread. But Philippine's letters confirmed that she was superior of a Missouri house that accepted at least one enslaved man in lieu of tuition and that later purchased an enslaved couple. At least she said she never really wanted to own enslaved persons and I, then, like others writing about Philippine, thought it meant that she knew the institution of slavery was fundamentally wrong. I found it painful but critically important while writing some 150 years later, long after the Civil War and Emancipation and on the heels of the U.S. civil rights movement, to condemn her involvement in the heinous practice of slavery.

And there was context. Most lighter-skinned "white" people where the religious lived had few or no qualms about slavery. Philippine's superiors, out of an interest in protecting the sensibilities of white parents, counseled her not to accept people of color into the order or the order's schools. They would lose (white) students. Even so, Philippine herself occasionally raised doubts about the systemic racism pervading the United States. She once suggested another white nun get on the first boat back to France after she objected to working in a laundry alongside enslaved black women. Barred from the more elite boarding schools, some mestizo and mulatto (but not black) girls were admitted to the day school despite racial prejudice. Philippine occasionally entertained circuitous strategies for women of color to enter religious life, albeit in a segregated status. Late in life Philippine got the chance to follow her deepest missionary calling when she was able to live for a time among the Potawatomi people. Too frail to do much, she earned their affection and the poignant title "Woman-Who-Prays-Always." For her part, she said some of them were saints, an opinion she also voiced also regarding other people of color, including mestizos and blacks.

The mixture of Philippine's striking sanctity and unwitting collusion with racial oppression were putting wrinkles in the "great woman" story I had hoped to write, but the wrinkles themselves were adding texture and depth to my appreciation for her. From hero to human, ideal to real, the Saint was becoming more like a sister.

Phase 3. Fast forward to the twenty-first century. It is 2018 as I write this reflection, the Bicentennial of Philippine's arrival in North America with four other Religious of the Sacred Heart. There are celebrations and commemorations. In the publication of Philippine's writings and other historical research, one finds again the Philippine who occasionally but persistently questioned aspects of the racist system in which she was enmeshed.

But there are further signs of her own racial prejudice and her acceptance of the oppression of people of color. She notes that enslaved persons are lazy and unreliable, that mixing white with indigenous or black blood produces children more inclined to evil. Philippine and her sisters subjected one enslaved woman, characterized as "bad" and prone to "incendiary remarks," to a few days in prison and the threat of the whip. Philippine indeed proffers many reasons for not wanting to own enslaved persons, but never once is it because she sees that slavery in and of itself is wrong.[31] She came from a socially-stratified French culture that didn't envision social mobility. She lived (and obeyed) a Catholic Church that, from popes in Rome to bishops in North America, condemned the harshest features of slavery and the ongoing enslavement of Africans, but did not condemn the trade or employment of already enslaved black people (or their children yet to be born).

But, fortuitously, in tandem with the Bicentennial, a constellation of new movements is pressing people, especially white people, to think more deeply about racism, a system that conspires, in insidious ways too little noticed by whites, to give more advantages to lighter- than darker-skinned people. Today, even as we carefully consider Philippine within her own historical context, it is crucial to recognize that any attempt to soft-pedal slavery is special pleading. Rationalizations along the lines of "everyone accepted it back then" (enslaved people? abolitionists?) amount to contorted attempts to justify a brutal, dehumanizing, and evil institution.

And, my relationship with Philippine today? Just as it was easy years ago to wholly sanctify Saint Philippine, so today it would be easy to wholly demonize her. But it is wholly unfair to impose present-day standards on people of the past. For all the evil of slaveholding, Philippine cannot be reduced to "slaveholder." It is certainly significant that Philippine's own descendants, her "daughters" in a sense, the Religious of the Sacred Heart, are themselves probing and making their history known, finding and contacting the descendants of the enslaved women and men who helped them build the Society of the Sacred Heart in North America, and struggling as individuals and through their institutions to establish racial justice.

Philippine's humility, sometimes exaggerated, was deep and true nonetheless. The generosity and zeal that impelled her to cross an ocean to educate girls of many classes and colors cannot be denied. The doubts that led her periodically to wonder how people of color might be admitted to her order or the order's schools suggests an individual receptive to the intuitions of her own conscience. Like all lives, hers was a complex amalgam of good and evil with, I note, the former in ascendancy.

Reflecting today on Philippine's blindness to slavery's evil, I, with my own history of entanglements with good and evil, can only wonder about my own blind spots. If a saint could not see that slavery was wrong, what might I, a more ordinary mortal, be missing?

---

31 I have incorporated some of this information in a Spanish translation of my 1990 book noted above, but more work remains to be done; see *Filipina Duchesne: Una Mujer con los Pobres y Marginados*, 2d. ed., revised and expanded, trans. María de los Ángeles Garriga González, with Clara Malo, RSCJ and Catherine M. Mooney (Kit, forthcoming 2018).

While it can be easy for white people to denounce and then distance ourselves from gross and overt expressions of racism, it is difficult to delve into our deeper spaces—personal, institutional, and societal—to discover and then expose unwitting collusions with both the benefits that racism affords the lighter-skinned and the damages it inflicts upon the darker-skinned.

Philippine is, perplexingly, saint, slaveholder and—still—sister. I cannot help but believe that were Philippine alive today, awakening along with other white people to the evils of slavery and its ongoing trail of racial injustices, she would be the first on the front lines, a pioneer once again, but this time crossing boundaries—no, rather, striking down boundaries that have cordoned off skin colors, privileging some over others.

Meditation on Philippine Duchesne

Madeleine Sophie Cooney, RSCJ

If Rose Philippine Duchesne were among us today,
living in a small community,
with a new kind of freedom to be creative,
innovative,
venturesome,
what would she do?
How would she mold and form her free choices?

Would she, for example, gather together some friends of like temper,
collect food, clothing, money,
lease a plane,
fly to Nicaragua to minister to the hungry
        to the illiterate
        to the victims of civil war?
Would she be another Mother Teresa—undoubtedly without the Nobel Prize?

Would she envision a house of prayer established in a space station?

How would she involve herself   in the peace movement
                           in women's issues
                           in initiatives for justice
                           in sanctuary
                           in bread for the world?

Would she live out great dreams of establishing the Kingdom of God
    in a renewal and refreshmentof education, of law, of politics, of economics,
    in a revival of parish life, of communication and the media,
    in pastoral ministry exercised in hospitals, among the poor,
        among intellectuals, artists, prisoners, students,
        alcoholics, victims of the drug culture,
        those dying of AIDS?

What challenges would she offer in community?
    How would she animate a common study of the Constitutions?
    How would she foster community discernment?

What kinds of breakthroughs would she achieve in relationships?

What creative forms would her loyalty to the Society take?

How would she relate in her personal life
    the values of being to those of becoming
    the values of tradition to those of evolution
    the values of permanence and stability to those of process and flexibility
    the values of being a Pilgrim of the Absolute to those of being a citizen of
    the world of relativity?

It could be argued that Philippine was a far more complex and imaginative
person than her behavior would indicate.

We have always to remind ourselves that she spoke and acted within the categories of the nineteenth century, in the confining vocabulary of contemporaneous
spirituality.

Therefore, we must read between the lines.
Above all, we must observe her actions and, perhaps even more,
    her refraining from action, her passion—
    what she did and what she suffered
        accepted
        dreamed
        aspired to
        counted as dross.

Women of the Frontier

Mary Pat White, RSCJ
November 18, 2006

WHEN I THINK OF Philippine today, I think of two titles dear to all of us: "A Woman of the Frontier" and "The Woman Who Prays Always." I want to share some thoughts with regard to these two aspects of our sister Philippine, hoping they will spark your own reflections about her. It seems meaningful to me at this juncture in our history to go back and understand her again from the point of view of being of the "frontier" because we, too, in the province today are surely at a very important Frontier Moment in our history.

We are preparing for an assembly-chapter this summer. We have completed twenty-five years as one province in the U.S. and now we look to the future. We have been a part of huge changes in the Society: its structure, its membership, how it sees itself as much more than RSCJ but embracing our Associates, our schools, our extended Sacred Heart Family.

Being of the frontier, of course, is hard because we're standing on a threshold. We're pointed towards the future but we're in the present. We know that there is something amazing, something unknown out there. We're moving towards it.

Are we frightened?

Are we drawn forward? Attracted?

Attracted! That surely was our Philippine! She was in France attracted to the missions in the New World. She was in Saint Charles but being drawn to Sugar Creek, Kansas. Then she was in Sugar Creek writing to Sophie that she felt that she should be moving on to the Rockies! She tells Sophie that people live to be a 100 there! (Where did she get that idea?)—And since she was just in her 70's, she figured that she had many years ahead of her to serve. This is so typical of her great-hearted generosity!

Truly she was the one who serves, the servant that John speaks of in our gospel today.

The poet David Whyte has a wonderful poem, which, I think, can guide our reflection this evening as we envision ourselves being "of the frontier." It is entitled, "Sometimes."

Sometimes
if you move carefully
through the forest

breathing
like the ones
in the old stories

who could cross
a shimmering bed of leaves
without a sound,

you come
to a place
whose only task

is to trouble you
with tiny
but frightening requests

conceived out of nowhere
but in this place
beginning to lead everywhere.

Requests to stop what
you are doing right now,
and

to stop what you
are becoming
while you do it,

questions
that can make
or unmake
a life,

questions
that have patiently
waited for you,

questions
that have no right
to go away.

These questions that have no right to go away, that have been waiting patiently for us—what are they? What are the questions being asked by the next new territory that is opening up in our lives, in the Society and, personally, in our own lives?

They are questions for sure that bring us into conversation with our suffering world, questions that make us terribly vulnerable.

Questions whose answers might just catch us off guard and blow our hearts entirely open.

Questions that will move us ahead in some unexpected ways. Risky questions that rise up from the whimpering of starving children, dying children.

Questions that come to us out of the shame of sex-trafficked children and women.

Questions that come to us in the moans and laments of all those whose loved ones have been blown up by suicide bombers in Iraq, Afghanistan, Israel, and Palestine; those whose loved ones have been humiliated and tortured by American military personnel.

Questions about how we are going to do our part in making the UN Millennium Goals a reality by 2015.

These are questions, and you will think of your own, that "make us stop what we are doing right now" in our lives and "stop what we are becoming while we are doing it," as David Whyte says.

These "questions that are not going to go away"—nor do we want them to—these are questions that "seem to come out of nowhere" but will truly "lead us everywhere," come out of our prayer and lead us to our own frontiers. These are questions that will keep us on the edge, keep us forever on the frontiers of our lives.

The second title of Philippine familiar to us is one that was given to her by the Potawatomi children in Sugar Creek. They put kernels of corn on her dress when they went to bed at night as she knelt in adoration in the tiny chapel. And in the morning, there they were, pretty much in the same place as the night before. Hence the title: "The Woman Who Prays Always."

Don't you wonder what it was that she did for eight hours in silence and solitude? Because she had obviously taken the Potawatomi into her care in the course of everyday activities, mending their clothes and doing other small menial tasks, I would imagine that she held them in her care in prayer as well. I think it was a spiritual motherhood that she exercised all night long, a motherly vigil.

This past summer during my retreat I listened to tapes by John O'Donohue, of Anam Cara fame. He was talking about the power of prayer and the Celtic tradition of taking people, of having people, in your care. For example, you might be responsible, make yourself responsible for them. They are in your care spiritually. You hold them with love and compassion in the presence of God. O'Donohue uses the term, "mind them." It is such a motherly sounding phrase, "to mind them," the kind of watchfulness and awareness that mothers have towards their children while the children are at play or asleep—perhaps totally unaware of their mothers.

I like to think that this is what Philippine was doing in all those hours in the presence of the Blessed Sacrament. And I like to think that we too, we who were of her frontier, her future, were also in her prayer—all of us, all unknown to her, who were to come to the Society really because of her—because of her courage, her zeal, her generosity, her prayer.

She was the single grain of wheat that bore the great harvest mentioned in our scripture today. O'Donohue talks about the level of prayer in the world, increased by the quiet, hidden prayer like Philippine's, those who spend hours holding the world in the embrace of love of the Heart of God. These are those, he says, who save the world from actually totally falling apart.

Sophie said: "It is not for ourselves that we should try to become interior souls. We should have constantly before our eye the children who come to claim spiritual help from us; the help that without prayer we shall never be able to give."

And so, in our year of prayer, let us be challenged to be women, using the image of David Whyte, who "move so quietly through the forest" as to be able to cross the thresholds, cross the thresholds of prayer without a sound and bring to the world that contemplative gaze of the mother minding her children, like Philippine in nightly vigil minding those who were in her care.

And let us meet the challenge of holding both the beauty and the violence of our world in deep awareness and attentiveness, in quiet mindfulness.

I wonder how being constantly on the frontier in her prayer and in her geography, how did that change Philippine from the person she would have become had she remained in France. Or in 1842, stayed in St. Charles How will being on our frontier change us too? We know that in the end it drained her of all her energy and strength even as she continued to give herself to it with such passion.

Let us ask our sister Philippine to show us how we, today, are to be "Women of the Frontier." How we too are to give ourselves to the new frontiers in our lives and in the depths of prayer with her kind of passion.

Openness to God

Maureen Glavin, RSCJ
2017

IN THIS REFLECTION, I am going to focus on what I see as one of Philippine's characteristics—her openness. That characteristic is one which her biographers do not usually mention. More often than not she is described with adjectives such as humble, compassionate, courageous and generous. My thesis is that these and other of her many admirable qualities flow from what I see as a this more primary interior attitude.

I offer three directions of openness for your consideration. These three directions fit into a paradigm which some thinkers and theologians have begun to use to talk about aspects of the Divine or the three faces of God. (See philosopher Ken Wilber for references to the Three Faces of Spirit; *Integral Spirituality* is a good source. A thorough Christian development of these ideas by Paul Smith can be found in his book *Integral Christianity*.)

The Three Faces of God

The first face of God is the God we meet within. This is the experience of God whom we discover at the depth of our Being. This is the encounter with the great "I AM" of God in whose image we are. This is the connection with God at the Ground of our Being, the Spirit within us or our Christ-nature. It is the God who is one with our authentic and deepest self. This face of God is the God we have come to know in interior prayer, in union and in communion.

The second face of God is the God we meet in others. This is the experience of God whom we discover in those before us. This is the encounter with the one who is in those we greet, work with, live with and meet daily. This is the connection with the God we experience in relationship. This is the face of Christ in our neighbor, in the poor, in the person of Jesus, and in the face of all those around us.

The third face of God is the God we meet in the physical world around us. This is the experience of God who is in all that is. This is the encounter with the one who is in the

— 158 —

stars, in the beauty of Creation, in the glory of nature, in the variety of colors, the diversity of species, the complexity of the Krebs Cycle and the functionality of a mitochondria. This is the connection with God who is the energy of the sun and in the process of evolution from the Big Bang to self-reflectively conscious stardust otherwise known as *homo sapiens*.

My thesis about Philippine is this: I contend that Philippine was amazingly open to God in each of these areas. I contend that she was wholeheartedly open to God within her, God before her and God around her. Let's look at each arena, in turn.

Openness to the God Within-Us

As mentioned, being open to the God-Within-US, i.e., that deep place within oneself, in silence brings one, over time, to a place of union with the Creator of the Universe. Being able to be quiet with oneself, being able to connect at one's depth, brings one to a place where one's own "I" and God's "I" are in union.

Philippine had an amazing inner connection with the Source of all Life and Love. Stories about this aspect of her are legend. During time she spent in prayer she was open to God, sitting with her Beloved, allowing herself to be suffused with, surrounded by, soaked in and nurtured by Love's Very Self. The *woman who prayed always* wasn't spending hours giving God God's to-do list for the day. She was loving and being loved. For that to happen she had to have been interiorly open. We describe it as her prayerfulness, but it was that interior openness which is the characteristic that fueled her life. I have been known to "sit" on my prayer cushion for an hour and think about what I needed to get at the grocery store, but, until I personally make the choice to open my heart to God, time on my prayer cushion is just time spent spinning my wheels. That interior openness is the road to union with God. God is always there loving us. Our choice is to be open. Once we choose that, prayer becomes less chatter and more Encounter. To discover God in prayer and contemplation, in the silence of our hearts, is, in fact, the core of Sacred Heart Spirituality.

The effect of being open to the God-Within is courage. Because of her interior contemplative connection with God, Philippine had amazing courage. Examples of this are also legend. Philippine returned to Grenoble during the dangerous years of the French Revolution; she visited priests when she could have been killed for helping them; she crossed an ocean in a little ship at the age of 48, left her family and friends and financial security to begin in a new place with few resources and lack of language. Her whole life, it seems to me, was one courageous act after another.

Openness to the God-Before-Us:

Being open to the God-Before-Us, i.e., others, expands one's sense of self to include the other, ultimately expanding it to a place of union with others. Our self-sense is developmental.

When we are little, it is all about us. As we grow, we begin to have the capacity for expanded circles of connection and empathy with others. At first it might just be with mommy. For example, when mommy hurts, I hurt. As we grow, that capacity expands to include others in our family. At one point, we begin to empathize with (include) those who are our friends, or maybe then to include those who look like us, those in our religion or those in our country. Have you ever noticed how easy it was to empathize with those in Florida and Houston who were struggling because of the recent hurricanes? Or, for those of you who are old enough, do you remember how our hearts ached when we sat in front of the TV watching the buildings in New York fall on 9/11? They were like us. We ached at their ache. How much more difficult that is to do when it is someone suffering or hurting in North Korea or Syria or Ethiopia? This capacity for openness to increasing circles of inclusion can be stated as moving from "me" to "us" to "all of us."

Regarding Philippine, she was so open to others, she ached not only when the children of Grenoble (her home town) were aching, she ached for the native children in a place that was very different from hers. From this globally inclusive heart flowed her desire to be with and work with and for the indigenous Americans and, I believe, it fueled her reverence for every "other" before her. From her writing we know that she also ached for those even farther afield—those in the Rocky Mountains farther West and even farther, those in China and Japan. Philippine was amazingly open to the Face of God, the Face of Christ, in others, no matter how "other" the "other" was. I believe she had a heart that encompassed the globe.

The effect of being open to the God before one, in front of one, being open to the God we meet in others leads to compassion. Moreover, the more open we are, the wider our circles of compassion.

There is an image of Philippine hanging outside of the chapel at Villa Duchesne and Oak Hill School in St. Louis, Missouri, which depicts these two mentioned aspects of Philippine's openness. In the painting, one of Philippine's hands is open to Christ—depicting her contemplative openness, her openness to the God she met in prayer, the God she met within. Her other hand is open to some members of the Potawatomi nation—depicting her openness to the other, to others, to her neighbor, her openness to the God she met in the face of those before her, especially those she felt were most in need.

Openness to the God-Around-Us

Finally, being open to God-Around-Us, in the exterior world, is not something that Philippine talked about so much, but I can't imagine her not experiencing that face of the Divine. It is however something that Pope Francis talks about. He invites us to be open to all of creation, the whole of the exterior world, and to see the Face of God in all of Creation. God is incarnate in the person of Jesus and through the revelation of that incarnation, we come to know something about all of creation. In the beginning was the Word and the Word became ... the Universe. A Cosmic Christology, which is part of our faith, is to understand that all of creation is a manifestation of the divine.

The effect of seeing God in the exterior world brings us to a place of awe and wonder. It also fuels curiosity for truth and in learning about the world: learning how the world operates, learning about how the world evolved, learning the relationship between matter and energy and what matter is made of and how it became more complexly arranged over time so that matter could be self-reflective once neo-cortexes were developed, learning where this planet, which we call earth, is located in relation to the stars in the Milky Way galaxy and how the energy of the sun gets turned into the chemical energy we eat and how that chemical energy is used to power our bodies, etc., etc., etc. As we grow in our understanding of all of this (and more) we will indeed be awed by the gloriousness, wondrousness and mysteriousness of it all, especially as we awaken to the Truth that the Glory and Wonder and Mystery is nothing less than the face of Christ around us!

Our Call:

So, this year, this bicentennial anniversary year of Sacred Heart education in what has become the United States Canada Network of Sacred Heart Schools, this anniversary year of Philippine's arrival to the Western Hemisphere, this anniversary year of the Society of the Sacred Heart and Schools of the Sacred Heart being global organizations, I think we have a clarion call. Our call, the call from Philippine's life and my invitation to all of us is to make the choice to be wholeheartedly OPEN!

First and foremost, I invite you to openness to that deep place inside—to take the journey to **God-within-you.** Next, I invite you to openness to those who are increasingly different—to take the journey to **God-before-you.** And, finally, I invite you to openness to understanding our world, our universe, and all of creation—to take the journey to **God-around-you.**

This journey to God will have benefits that are bountiful! For, anyone who discovers God *within* themselves will live with more courage. Anyone who discovers God *before* themselves will live with more compassion. And, anyone who discovers God *around* them, will live with more curiosity.

Let us start by being open to discover God, and then, let us live lives that reveal God in our courage, our compassion and our curiosity.

May it be so, in the journey of this year and in the journey of our lives!

Author Biographies

Elaine Abels, RSCJ (1943-), a scientist by training, was for many years a hospital chaplain; she now ministers to the elderly and infirm at the Sarah Community in St. Louis, Missouri.

Maureen Aggeler (1938-), an educator and writer, is a former RSCJ who coordinated the Roman celebrations of the canonization of Philippine.

St. Madeleine Sophie Barat, RSCJ (1779-1865), founder of the Society of the Sacred Heart, received Philippine into the Society and served as superior general throughout Philippine's lifetime; her friendship with Philippine is recorded in their many letters.

Catherine Baxter, RSCJ (1928-2009), was headmistress at both Newton Country Day School of the Sacred Heart and Carrollton School of the Sacred Heart; she served also as director of the community at Oakwood, the Society's retirement center in Atherton, California.

Eileen Bearss, RSCJ (1924-), gave many years of service to the Society in financial administration.

Rosemary Bearss, RSCJ (1931-), was provincial of the United State Province, 1988-1994, formerly business manager of Duchesne College, Omaha, and director of the Barnyard, a project for children and young people in Miami.

Gertrude Bodkin, RSCJ (1875-1966), from Ireland, was sent to the United States in 1909 to be mistress of novices; she continued in that role until 1931 when she was named vicar in the East of the United States, a role she held for more than twenty years.

Beverly Boyd (1925-) is professor emerita of English at the University of Kansas and a poet; a devotee of Saint Philippine, she celebrates the saint's story in her poetry.

Meg Huerter Brudney is the head of school at Duchesne Academy of the Sacred Heart, Omaha, of which she is an alumna.

Walter J. Burghardt, SJ (1914-2008), was a well known advocate of social justice and ecumenism, about which he wrote and preached widely.

Annice Callahan, RSCJ (1945-), is a retired professor of theology in both Canada and the U.S. She has also done pastoral and retreat work.

Jane Cannon, an alumna of Maryville, is a former teacher and staff member at the Academy of the Sacred Heart, St. Charles, the history of which she has written as part of the commemoration of the Academy's bicentennial.

Tara L. Carnes teaches at the Regis School of the Sacred Heart in Houston, Texas; she is a musician, composer, poet, teacher, and spiritual director.

Madeleine Sophie Cooney, RSCJ (1912-1994), was a professor of humanities at Duchesne College, Omaha, and at Barat College; her special gift was the integration in her teaching of the various disciplines of art history, history, philosophy, and theology.

Margaret Conroy, RSCJ (1930-), from Canada, has served as a missionary for more than forty years in the Province of Uganda/Kenya, of which she was provincial.

Peter De Smet, SJ (1801-1873), came from Belgium as a missionary to Louisiana; he evangelized several nations of Native Peoples as far as the Pacific Coast.

Therese Downey, RSCJ (1927-2017), spent many years teaching elementary school children in Network schools and in other schools and educational settings with which the Society is connected, including Thensted Center in Grand Coteau, Louisiana.

Jan Dunn, RSCJ (1946-), has served in a variety of roles in the Network of Sacred Heart Schools, including headmistress of two schools, as well as board member of others, and interim director of the Network.

Sally M. Furay, RSCJ (1926-2015), was dean and provost at the University of San Diego and active in consulting at various colleges, universities, and other educational institutions.

Maureen Glavin, RSCJ (1959-), is an educator in the Network of Sacred Heart Schools who recently served as head of school at the Academy of the Sacred Heart in St. Charles, Missouri; she is currently a member of the USC province leadership team.

Melanie Guste, RSCJ (1952-), after several years as an independent educational and organizational consultant, is serving now as headmistress of The Rosary in New Orleans, of which she is an alumna.

Kathleen Hughes, RSCJ (1942-), a native of Cleveland, spent nineteen years teaching liturgy, sacraments and preaching at the Catholic Theological Union in Chicago, followed by six years as provincial of the United States Province.

Sharon Karam, RSCJ (1944-), from Louisiana, is a long-time Network educator; she has served in administrative and teaching roles, most recently as teacher of English and service coordinator at Duchesne Academy Houston.

Bonnie Kearney, RSCJ (1943-), is a long-time educator who spent many years in schools for marginalized children; she currently ministers at the Duchesne House for Volunteers in New Orleans, Louisiana.

Jeanne Legrelle, RSCJ (1916-2010), was a middle school teacher and later a treasurer in houses of the Province of France.

Clare McGowan, RSCJ (1927-1993), was an educator at both college and secondary level; she served as education director of the Washington Vicariate and as headmistress of Stone Ridge School of the Sacred Heart.

Helen McLaughlin, RSCJ (1932-), was a missionary in Uganda where she was provincial, then representative of Africa at the motherhouse; in 1982, she was elected superior general of the Society of the Sacred Heart, serving in that role until 1994. She continues to give retreats and spiritual direction.

Shirley Miller, RSCJ (1940-), served as teacher and administrator in several Sacred Heart schools before becoming mission advancement director of the United States-Canada Province.

Mary Moeschler, a Network educator, served as head of the middle school at Forest Ridge School of the Sacred Heart and also taught at Duchesne Academy of the Sacred Heart in Omaha, Nebraska.

Catherine Mooney (1952-), a professor of Church History at Boston College, is author of a biography of Philippine Duchesne and lectures and writes about other saints, especially from the medieval period.

Juliet Mousseau, RSCJ (1979-), is a professor of Church History at the Aquinas Institute of Theology in St. Louis, Missouri.

Odeide Mouton, RSCJ (1896-1993), was president of Maryville College and later headmistress of Stone Ridge School of the Sacred Heart, Bethesda, Maryland.

John Courtney Murray, SJ (1904-1967), was a theologian remarkable for his liberal thought, especially in church-state relations; a *peritus* at the Second Vatican Council, he was responsible for drafting the Council's document on religious freedom.

Marcia O'Dea, RSCJ (1938-), has taught English literature and writing at Forest Ridge School of the Sacred Heart for more than forty years.

Nance O'Neil, RSCJ (1928-), served as provincial treasurer in New York and then as first provincial of the United States Province; she initiated the foundation of the Society in Indonesia.

Carol Purtle (1939-2008), a graduate of both Maryville and Manhattanville and a former RSCJ, was an art historian with recognized expertise in Netherlandish art.

Denise Pyles (1964-) is a pastoral minister as well as a musician and composer who has produced recordings of original music, including two songs for the Society and the Network, and two volumes of poetry and memoirs.

Rose Marie Quilter, RSCJ (1936-), taught and practiced therapeutic massage before beginning her current ministry, Dreams Without Borders, at ARISE in the Rio Grande Valley, where she conducts classes in alternative health and basic English to adult immigrants.

Barbara Quinn, RSCJ (1948-), is at present the associate director for spiritual formation at the Boston College School of Theology and Ministry; her ministries have included formation, spiritual direction and retreat work, teaching and adult spiritual development.

Marie Louise Schroen, RSCJ (1909-1991), was mistress of novices for the United States and Canada and later mistress of the international probation; during her last years, she taught Scripture to both lay and religious groups in the United States and around the world.

Mary Schumacher, RSCJ (1941-), spent many years in parish ministry and counseling; at present she facilitates retreats and gives spiritual direction.

Carmen Smith, RSCJ (1920-2003), a poet and teacher, served the educational mission of the Society in classrooms of the Southern Province for more than fifty years.

Frances Tobin, RSCJ (1934-), was a middle school teacher and counselor in her earlier years; after obtaining a law degree, she has practiced immigration law and other forms of social ministry.

Judy Vollbrecht, RSCJ (1940-), is an anthropologist who worked in Africa for some time; she was one of the founders of the Society's mission in Haiti.

Elizabeth Walsh, RSCJ (1933-2017), was a literary scholar and professor of English at the University of San Diego, where she also taught a course in the history of the Society of Jesus and the Society of the Sacred Heart.

Archbishop Thomas Wenski (1950-), appointed archbishop of Miami since 2010, spent many years in ministry to Hispanic and Haitian communities; he recently spoke out strongly on the issue of gun violence.

Mary Pat White, RSCJ (1942 -), who has served in administration of Network schools and as a campus minister at university Newman Centers in California, is presently working with young adults in the Boston area.

Margaret Williams, RSCJ (1902-1996), was professor of English and American literature at Manhattanville College, a Middle English scholar and editor of major Anglo-Saxon and Middle English texts; she was also the author of biographies of Aloysia Hardey and Madeleine Sophie Barat.

CPSIA information can be obtained
at www.ICGtesting.com
Printed in the USA
FSHW010804190919
62157FS